First Dog on the Moon's
Guide to Living Through
the IMPENDING
APOCALYPSE
And how to stay nice doing it

Appropriate for
kids who like
swearing

ABC
Books

The ABC 'Wave' device is a trademark of the
Australian Broadcasting Corporation and is used
under licence by HarperCollinsPublishers Australia.

First published in Australia in 2017
by HarperCollinsPublishers Australia Pty Limited
ABN 36 009 913 517
harpercollins.com.au

theguardian

First Dog on the Moon is a beloved cartoonist for Guardian Australia,
where some of the material in this book first appeared. You can read the
hilarious cartoons at theguardian.com/au

HarperCollinsPublishers
Level 13, 201 Elizabeth Street, Sydney NSW 2000, Australia
Unit D1, 63 Apollo Drive, Rosedale, Auckland 0632, New Zealand
A 53, Sector 57, Noida, UP, India
1 London Bridge Street, London, SE1 9GF, United Kingdom
2 Bloor Street East, 20th floor, Toronto, Ontario M4W 1A8, Canada
195 Broadway, New York, NY 10007, USA

National Library Library of Australia Cataloguing-in-Publication data:
First Dog on the Moon, author, illustrator.
First Dog's guide to living through the impending apocalypse and
how to stay nice doing it / First Dog on the Moon.
9780733334252 (paperback)
9781460704967 (ebook)
End of the world–Humour.
End of the world–Pictorial works.
End of the world in art.
Apocalypse in art.
Comic books, strips, etc.–Australia.
Australian wit and humor, Pictorial.

Cover and internal design by Jane Waterhouse
Colour reproduction by Graphic Print Group, Adelaide
Printed and bound in China by RR Donnelley

6 5 4 3 2   19 20

For Bronte

Contents

The End

The REAL Contents

Chapter 1 - What is this terrible book?
Chapter 2 - Why would you write
a book this awful?
Chapter 3 - Even the pictures don't help
Chapter 4 - Oh god here is another chapter
Chapter 5 - And another
Chapter 6 - Where will it end?!
Chapter 7 - All the chapters after chapter 6
The End - Thank goodness
Epilogue - nooooooooo
Footnotes - erk

Foreword

When I stumbled across First Dog on the Moon's cartoons last year I fell into a goofball swoon. Who was this audacious young buck with the peculiar name, the swift pen, and such friendly but deadly aim?

You might even call it love, if it is possible for a cartoonist to love another cartoonist, which it isn't.

So let's dial back the emotion and just say I dig First Dog on the Moon like crazy. I dig him because First Dog on the Moon is the greatest pen-name in the history of art. I dig him because his drawings are as crude and bulgy-eyed as my own. I dig him because although he writes in Australian and I speak only Californian, I think I get half the references. I dig him because he gives public talks wearing a shark suit and never explains or even acknowledges this. And I dig First Dog on the Moon because he always makes me laugh.

This book is First Dog on the Moon at his best. It's a thoroughly unhelpful self-help book, combined with an utterly unreliable how-to guide, combined with a profusely illustrated cartoon book, jammed full of quips and japes and paradoxes and contradictions and footnotes and jokes. It's really about the stuff that keeps you awake at night, worrying and sweating and tossing and turning – you know: life, death, annihilation, darkness, and laughs. And I guarantee that wherever you think this book is going, you are going to be surprised – this book zigs just when you think it's going to zag. And I'm not kidding when I say that there are moments of grief and sadness amidst the satire and sight gags, and that in addition to the fun stuff there's some damn good politics and inspiration.

Plus did I mention the doom? First Dog says we're all doomed, probably.

Have fun!

Matt Groening, creator of *The Simpsons*

Mr Groening
by
F Onthemoon

Meet your new best friend F Onthemoon (Bestselling Author)

starring in

HOW I SURVIVED BEING A BEST SELLING AUTHOR

Welcome to First Dog on the Moon's Guide to Living Through the Impending Apocalypse. Here is a message from F Onthemoon.

> Hello I'm First Dog on the Moon, best-selling author and your new best friend.

HOW GOOD ARE BOOKS THOUGH!

Did you know I am a best selling author? It's true!* I have the credibility and gravitas that not being a best selling author doesn't give you. Accordingly, you can feel free to trust me the same way you would trust JK Rowling or the Bible. All bestsellers!

PREVIOUS BEST SELLING BOOK (WEIGHS A KILO!)

A Treasury of Cartoons by First Dog on the Moon

GET A BIG DOG

Best Selling Author

I haven't always been a Walkley award winning cartoonist and humble national treasure. Once upon a time like you I was a regular person with a job (in a call centre) and my life was an unending parade of despair as I lurched wretchedly from day to day just waiting to die.

Me

NATIONAL TREASURE

You (formerly me)

CUSTOMERS ROCK!

But now due to hard work and talent I am a famous and adorable celebrity. It is pretty great. While this book won't make you famous or interesting like me it may just save your life!**

Book you are reading right now

First Dog On the Moon's Guide to Living Through the IMPENDING APOCALYPSE AND HOW TO STAY NICE DOING IT

Fact and fun filled

Contains true tales of survival!!

Awesome book

Moi

← Not having a midlife crisis or any sort of breakdown

You may be wondering how I am qualified to to guide you on our perilous yet exciting journey through this possibly life-saving book** (which I am confident will also be a best-seller.)

Truth be told I am not.

akubra bought at airport

burns easily

military grade spork

soft hands

bag contains: ipad laptop back up ipad apple pencil glasses cleaner paw paw ointment

But that doesn't matter. What's important is that every single one of the hand-curated hints, suggestions and clever ideas in this book comes with the stamp of 100% Guaranteed Internet Accuracy.

THE INTERNET IS NEVER WRONG

> And as you know by now, you can trust me!

I ♥ BEST SELLING AUTHORS

Please enjoy this book. You're welcome!

* That is why I am allowed to put it on my business card
** It will not save your life (Please see page 191)

What is this book?

Gentle reader, you hold in your tiny furry paws...

...the most important book you will ever read (unless you don't read in which case you're holding the most important book you won't ever read but don't know that because you don't read ever).

Already so many questions! Why is this book so important? Why do you have tiny furry paws? The world is a terrible place yet also filled with wonder and joy, and we don't even know the half of it, but if it is so great, why are we trying to ruin it to death and kill all the people and the animals? Already so many questions and many more will be answered within these pages. Or will they? Yes they will. See! We have started already.

What a pickle we find ourselves in, what a self-brining species we are. Here we have the end of the world looming and how are we responding? By drinking cups of tea and complaining about it on the internet.

It must be said that for some folk the world is already terrible and they don't even have cups of tea or the internet in their country how awful how does this book help them I hear you ask? Don't be so smug, of course it doesn't. This book is for the comfortably unready. It is a book for glossy arts administrators like you and your turmeric-sprinkled barista friends. If I wanted to write a book that was useful for everyone on Earth all at once it would be a pamphlet on hygiene available in Esperanto. And frankly I don't appreciate the tone of your question.

You
↓

me not appreciating the tone of your question

Ask yourself how you will survive an asteroid strike, a global pandemic or an electromagnetic pulse? You will not. Unless you read this book but even then you still might not make it. It is probably time to formulate some sort of plan. Fortunately for you I have been looking at the website 'google' on the internet.

Within these pages you will find everything you need to prepare for surviving the end of the world[1] just like a 'prepper'. But make sure you read all of it right away (after buying copies for your loved ones and 'friends') because you will be far too busy to read it when you are running to your hastily dug fallout-proof bunkers to hide from whichever apocalyptic evil ultimately shows up.

Apocalyptic evil example 1

WHO ARE PREPPERS AND WHY DO WE CARE?

Humans have been preparing and not preparing for the worst for as long as there have been humans and the worst. It is a natural human trait to under or over compensate and then laugh with your mates at the people who aren't doing it like you. It is fun to mock and jeer but who will be laughing when the Yellowstone supervolcano erupts destroying the USA and resulting in an ELE? Not you because you probably don't even know what ELE stands for and you're certainly not ready for the subsequent 20-year ice age that follows it I'm not even joking.

The most exciting preppers (I'm generalising a teeny bit) live in the USA and tend to be hard-right evangelist Christian types with a profound distrust of government and an enormous enthusiasm for the Second Amendment. Preppers have a lot of guns. Everyone in America has a lot of guns but preppers have more. They think the government/United Nations/jihadis/feminists will be coming for their guns soon and they want to be ready and for the most part they are extremely ready so avoid them.

They also know a great deal about what to do if/when the end of the world shows up and it would all be hilarious except the world probably is going to end so we shall pinch their ideas while laughing at them isn't this fun? If you're prepping in Australia it is pretty much the same as the USA except with fewer guns and more space and way more spiders. Australia and the USA are about the same size one has 320 million people and the other has 24 million you do the mathification. If you're in the UK keep calm and etc. If you're anywhere else good luck don't come to Australia we will put you in a death camp.

So welcome to this book which I have written solely for the purpose of helping you and your family stay safe when the impending apocalypse arrives it has nothing to do with wanting to get invited to writers' festivals. Don't mention it. Please don't read the fine print which is down the back.[2]

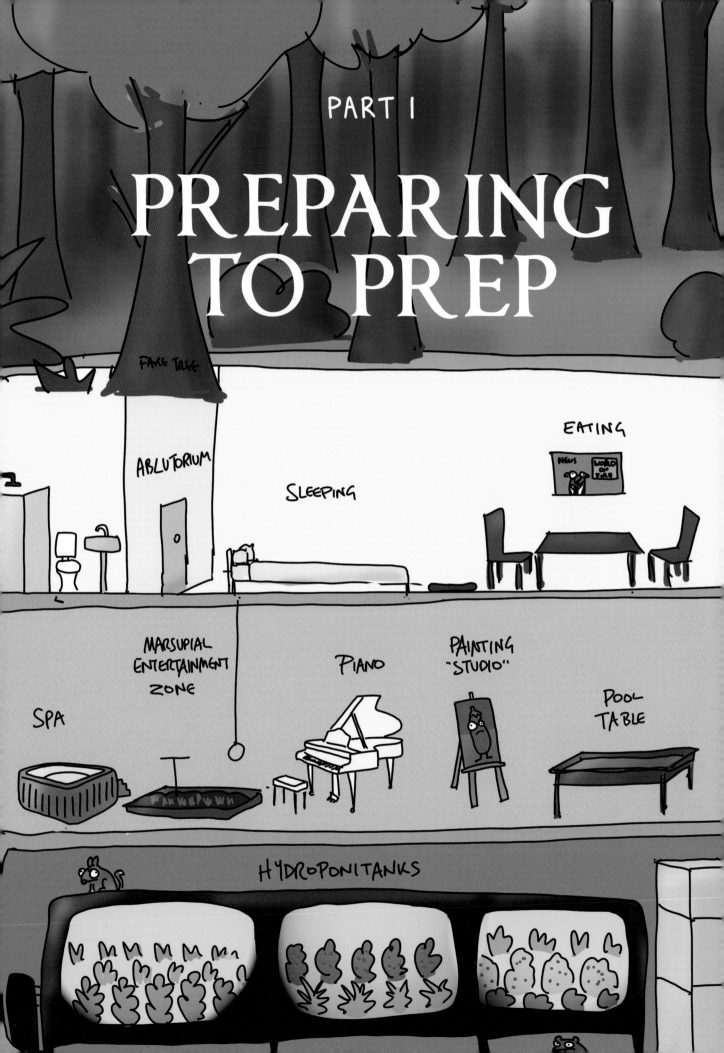

CHAPTER 1

Welcome to prepping: what even is it?

Welcome to the exciting life of a prepper and THE END OF THE WORLD AS WE KNOW IT (TEOTWAWKI)

What does one do when, as the Americans say – the SHTF – when TEOTWAWKI arrives? We shall start with the basics. Do not run about with your undies on your head. It doesn't help now and it's not going to help at the end of the world.

Do not do this.

How does one respond to the imminent (results may vary) collapse of civilisation. Should you be stashing tins of tuna and chickpeas under the floorboards (yes) and squirrelling a shotgun away behind the pallet of Purity Weasel weightloss protein shakes in the shed? (no) Don't hide your shotgun in the shed carry it with you at all times. Hide it in your backpack unless you will be 'breaking' the 'law'. Of course we don't call it a backpack any more you're a prepper now it is a BOB or 'Bug Out Bag'.

And what specifically are we preparing for? All the electricity to die? Cows to take over the United Nations and implement a one world cowliphate? Ahahah see what I did there? The exciting thing about the looming end of the world is that WE DON'T ACTUALLY KNOW HOW OR WHEN IT IS GOING TO HAPPEN JUST THAT IT IS DEFINITELY CERTAINLY GOING TO HAPPEN IN AN EXTREMELY INCONVENIENT FASHION. This makes it a lot harder to plan for every eventuality. Yet here we are. Survivalism and Prepping (two different things FYI) are big business! A lot of people make a lot of money either preying on people's fears or selling them critical equipment they will need or both. It will help if you can spend millions of dollars on your prepping but we also cover 'Not dying on a budget'. Do you have access to any sort of spacecraft?

Even a small rocket like this one might come in very handy

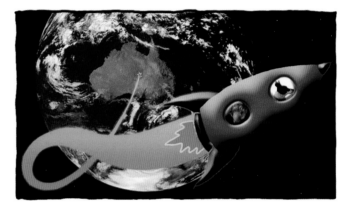

Have you heard of the rule of threes? We preppers have. A person can live 3 minutes without air, 3 hours without shelter, 3 days without water and 3 weeks without food. Also, 3 seconds without internet, 6 hours without patting a dog and 30 minutes without coffee after I wake up. These are approximations of course, just general guidelines because if something went horribly wrong for me and I got lost in the forest I would expect to last till about mid afternoon then they would find my corpse under a log or hiding under a badly collected pile of leaves from some poisonous shrub I thought might protect me from lightning or panthers or whatever kills people in the forest.

As discussed previously I'm not writing this book from the perspective of someone who knows what they are doing, just someone who had the foresight to look at a bunch of websites before the terrorists blew the up internet or it got lost in the forest on the way home and panthers ate it after it was hit by lightning. Anyway at some point we won't be able to google things any more, and then we will all just die like the old people did before the world wide web. (I think the 3 hours without shelter part of that rule, assumes you are stupid enough to be in the snow when the world ends. Or Queanbeyan.)

Sensible preppers DON'T wait until there are giant Nazi tapeworms roaming the streets, they 'prepare'. Now you can too! Remember, you can't expect to tootle in your Prius down to the local supermarket and buy a pallet of Purity Weasel Kale Filtered Spring Water because the supermarket will be on fire and it will have been looted. The only thing left will be a leaky six pack of Panicky Bob's Triple Caffeinated Activated Almond Power Drinkade Frappés

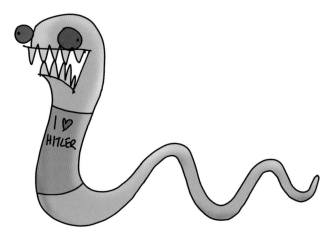

which you will have to fight an
axe-wielding former employee of
the Department of Veterans Affairs
for and they will probably take your
Prius and how will you get home to
your thirsty family who are probably
by now drinking guinea pig urine or something OH GOD YOU NEED
TO GET ORGANISED NOW!! IMAGINE CHRISTMAS SHOPPING EXCEPT
100 TIMES WORSE AND EVERYONE HAS AN AXE! That is what the
end of the world will be like.

Decision time! When it all goes horribly wrong you'll most likely have two
maybe three choices:

1. Bugging in – Assuming you have somewhere to live already, this is staying at home where all your things are, makes it much easier. But is it safe? No. Maybe. It depends.

2. Bugging out – This is basically running away – fleeing to your pre-arranged bug out location (BOL), the carefully selected secluded rural hideaway you prepared earlier. Don't have one? That's okay you would probably get smugged to death by a rabid herd of Young Liberals on the way there. It look's like you're bugging in unless...

3. What if you're not even at home so you don't have all your stuff – do you go home? Is it safe? Do you have an EDC[3]? No you don't because who does?! Are the trams running? YOUR TRAM APP WON'T BE WORKING. DO YOU KNOW WHERE YOUR PETS ARE?! OMG this is so complicated. There are so many things you have to think about perhaps it would just be easier to die when God's righteous but completely unprepared for and unexpected rain of boiling custard pours from the sky.

4. Freaking out and dying, or possibly hitting your head and waking up a couple of days later to find the world has been transformed into a sci-fi dystopia/utopia or maybe a cornucopia of on-going torment full of terrible things and dreadful people, i.e. nothing has changed.

Don't panic yet, we go into more detail about bugging in/and/or out later on.

So what should you do now?! Start getting ready first before you even know what to do here is what you should do read this next part straight away. But before we do that a word from our sponsor.

 FIRST DOG TRUE LIFE SURVIVAL STORIES! TRUE TALES OF SURVIVALIST DERRING DO FROM YOURS TRULY WRITER AND NATIONAL TREASURE F ONTHEMOON

TRUE LIFE SURVIVAL STORIES I

HOW I SURVIVED BEING BORN IN AUSTRALIA

Hello Australia, I have always loved you.

I even loved you that time I was clearing up the leaves from the banana tree in the back yard and the funnel web spider wanted to kill me. Have you ever seen a funnel web spider? They hate you and your way of life even if they have never met you. Always check your shoes before putting them on.

atrax robustus

One of the nicest things about being a cartoonist is coming up with stuff about the bad and dangerous creatures in Australia because I love it. Australia is full of racists (don't love those) velvety poisonous spiders (pro-spider as long as it is over there) giant prehistoric murder turkeys (would vote for them) and the sort of folk who like to dig holes for animals to fall into and all sorts of terrible rubbish (fire these people into the Sun). I love Australia in spite of the terrible, evil and poisonous gear strutting or scuttling about the landscape. I write and draw about the good things in Australia for the same reason. I love them too. All of it.

I love that my earliest memory of Australia is the ABC.[4] I am sitting in the kitchen in my childhood home in Bega, Dad is making Vegemite sandwiches for lunch and the ABC news theme comes on the radio. The kettle is boiling. I love the ABC too.

Walking through the bush when it is pushing 40 degrees and then standing still. I love how nothing moves in the heat along with the great roaring silence broken only by the slow, solemn tick of the eucalypts. The air is alive and thick with the smell of the gumtrees and the baking earth. The heat swallows you whole and the very air strives to push you into the ground. And with it always, the quiet looming menace of fire. Australia is always trying to kill you.

I love watching Test cricket. With the TV sound off and the ABC radio on.

I'm eating watermelon so cold it hurts my teeth. Out the window the sprinkler is on at the wrong time of day, in the heat, but it's in the backyard so we should be good as long as the neighbours don't hear it and dob us in over the water restrictions, they have theirs on often enough. (Not a true story of course.)

In these days of patriotism and plastic shopping bags blowing into the sea, the idea that there is an Australian way to do things means there is an un-Australian way to do things and who has time for that. I do not. The greater stick-nest rat* and the kookaburra** have no time for that.

Even so I love the people here, people who are at once warm and irreverent and intolerant and full of fear and perhaps a little hope. The broken, bitter, cold and cruel among us. The disempowered and the dispossessed. Each and every one. I love us all most days.

Geez we can be funny buggers though. I love that too. The way we talk, I reckon if the scientists could work out a way to weaponise an accent, Australian voices could blast a hole in the moon. Yeah, nah.

It is not always easy to love you Australia, it is a love that is bright and deep like your slowly poisoned oceans, I am struck down and left speechless so often by the cruelty and seemingly infinite capacity to turn away from the suffering of others, to block people out like we block out the brutal summers. Fearful, mistrustful, stifled and sweating in our lives apart. Claustrophobic, terrified of knowledge and kindness and death. We pride ourselves on our larrikin spirits all the while tut tutting and writing letters to the editor, 'Dear Sir/Madam, thayortadosomethn'.

Did you know that Aboriginal Australians were living in communities of up to 5,000 people before the colonisers came? They had storage for grain and farming and aquaculture did you know? It shouldn't matter if they did or they didn't, what matters is why don't 'we' know about it, why don't we want to know about it? I don't love that.

I do love our poisonous and venomous animals (not necessarily in person). I love the giant dinosaur cassowaries*** but the idea of them scares me. I love sharks. Funnel-web spiders**** are great. Then there are kookaburras. What a ridiculous and charming bird. We chose the emu***** but there are so many that could/should be our national bird. All of them. We should be governed by sulphur-crested cockatoos****** I love the light. And the clattering honking crunching cheeping rustling roaring sound of it all.

cacatua galerita

And public transport, our trams and trains make me want to cheer when they go past!

Yes, I know that lots of countries have public transport. But they don't have this landscape.
Or space.
The light.
The flora.
The fauna.
All of it, except the bits I don't like.
The wonderful terrible people.
Home.

* (*Leporillus conditor*)
** (*Dacelo novaeguineae*)
*** (*Casuarius casuarius*)
**** (*Atrax robustus*)
***** (*Dromaius novaehollandiae*)
****** (*Cacatua galerita*)

This picture of a sunfish doesn't really belong here but I like it a lot.

The Secret Prepper Poem

It's time that we all came to grips
with the looming apocalypse

Don't wait till the shit hits the fan,
you should already have a plan!

So heed this sensible advice,
make your list then check it twice

Then you should check it two times more,
wait what's that knocking at the door...

Giant peas from outer space!

Poison bees to eat your face!

All the things that you have missed,
because you didn't check your list.

You're dead and while it seems unfair,
it's your fault you did not prepare

CHAPTER 2

Let's get prepping!

First up it's time to make a list! We preppers love lists so much we even have a poem about it.

All preppers know this poem but of course if you ask them they will deny it. That's how you know someone is secretly prepping – if they pretend they do not know this poem THEY ARE ONE.

Ten critical things you must do in order to be ready to start preparing to be ready.

1. GET INFORMED!

Where to begin? Go and check out some prepping websites!

Ahahahaha no I'm just kidding don't do that those people are complicated and reality is a distant cousin they don't ever remember meeting. They are ready for anything but also unhinged. Just read this book, it contains everything you need (unless you think you need in-depth analysis of how the use of chemtrails will ensure the lizards in the United Nations can finally take over). If you finish this book and want to look in more detail, try some of the following books/sites.

— Chemtrails are the way the lizards in the United Nations are going to finally take over, Part 1, by Bradley 'Bugout' Bitoubusch.

— Prepping for the One World Caliphate, I'm not a racist you're a racist: Why my ex-wife won't let me see the kids. Mink Lithium.

– *I lived in a hole in the ground in the Wickatikitee Mountains for five years and you can too. Survival Darren.*

– *Home canning for fun, profit and the fiery damnation of the Lord. Claudette Orglette.*

– *No dentist, no doctor just a military grade spork and a steady hand: Home Surgery after the collapse. 'Dr' Calvin 'Salmonella' Sporran.*

– *Hand-to-hand fighting and vegetable gardening in containers. Amy Jo Poutine.*

2. DECIDE WHO IS ON YOUR PREPPING TEAM

Your first official task as a prepper is to decide who is on your PREPPING TEAM – if you are a family it can be easy – but what if it's not? Decide who will be a part of your plan and who won't.

Remember you might not like your housemate but a brain surgeon might be handy in a pinch. Cartoonists might not seem useful but they really can be also they are quiet and don't eat much.

It might seem strange to worry about your prepping team first but it could turn into your biggest mistake when a SHTF event really happens. If you don't watch what you say and do, and who you tell, you could be planning to support four people and end up with seventeen freeloaders to feed in an emergency. You will need to tell the right people about it IN SECRECY and get them involved – if you do it with the right levels of desperation and spittle-flecked enthusiasm with any luck, they will be so horrified they will move away and you won't have to worry about them. Don't tell anyone yet – finish reading this book first – and then you can explain to the people you have selected for your team how the hole you are digging in the backyard will be big enough to hide the whole crew and the post apocalyptic toilet system you have been working on here it is would you like to see how it works?

THIS IS IMPORTANT. DO NOT EVER TELL ANYONE YOU ARE A PREPPER BECAUSE WHEN THE WORLD ENDS THEY WILL COME TO YOUR HOUSE AND BASH YOU OVER THE HEAD WITH A SHOVEL. I AM NOT EVEN JOKING.

3. MAKE A LIST OF EVERYTHING YOU NEED

You need to make a list of all the things you need to do and get. It is important that while you are making it you are panicking that your list will not be comprehensive and you will miss something critical – add extra of everything. This is because you will be in constant state of panic when the world is ending so get used to it now.

Whether you decide to bug in or bug out (see next chapter) there are some things you will need irregardless, things that are non-negotiable because they are essential if you want TO LIVE. What a terrible sentence that was but see how easily distracted you are? Pay attention it could SAVE YOUR LIFE. This is the list of things that will be critical when TITWAKKA because it's like going camping but it lasts forever and people are trying to kill you.

the people you meet while camping for the rest of your life

Once you have everything on this list you will be able to survive pretty much anything except a direct hit from the sun.

Water

You will need a bunch of it. How much? Well that depends, do you pee a lot? Most people need three to four litres a day (which includes 'sanitation' and cooking) and you should have enough for at least three days so that is like twelve litres or something. A litre of water weighs a kilo, which is quite heavy if you have more than a few.

It all sounds like a lot. And don't forget your pets – and if one of your pets is a dolphin or something you are going to need a lot more – what if you have a thirsty rescue dog? This one time we had a cat with poor kidney function and the hairy thirsty bastard drank so much water all day long we got him a legit electricity-powered CAT FOUNTAIN. The water kept going all day – remember, these are just general guidelines – your specific requirements may be ridiculous so sort your shit out.

Food

How good is food though you will need enough for everyone or you will be hungry and how terrible would it be to starve to death like someone not in a Western country!? An 'average' adult needs about 8700kj a day and so do I.

Everything else

There are some other things you will need, including a way to cook all that food, matches or other ways to light a fire, fire, some pots and pans and so on, kitchen knives, a fork, teaspoons, a first aid kit, medicine, clothes, a raincoat but not an umbrella (too cumbersome), all sorts of different tools like hammers and screwdrivers and shovels and a big crowbar thing, a diesel generator, snow chains for your car, insect repellent, a radio, a sewing kit, pencils and paper, pet carrier, swim goggles (for chopping onions), crazy glue, batteries, a torch, nails and wood, soap, toothpaste, a mirror (for testing if anyone is a vampire also good for signalling), swiss army knife, cryptocurrency, bobby pins, paper clips, paper plates (avoid dishwashing), bicycle, a doona (for snuggling under), tent, barry pins, camping mattress, rope, cups to drink out of, shoes or boots, shoe or bootlaces, containers to store food in to protect them from rats and insects, toilet paper, feminine hygiene products, baby things if you have a baby or small children and are planning to take them with you, rescue-dog medicine if your dog has a dodgy ticker, ten different kinds of essential oils, gas mask, anti-radiation suit, iodine pills, buckets, bay leaves, black plastic sheeting, another bicycle, television remote control (to stare at wistfully whilst sitting by the fire), chicken, charcoal for curing food poisoning (also drawing tasteful nudes), precious metals (cash will be useless), clean underwear x 2, soldering iron, magnifying glass, elbow parts, tarps, water filter, salt, important personal documents, utility/rates bill for proof of residence, baking powder, laminating machine, squirrel trap, shotgun, squirrel, jacket, bumwizzle, cotton wool, vodka (for killing wasps and curing ear infections), duct tape (various colours), boffin detector, trebuchet, weevil mallet.

And most importantly – a lot of zip lock bags.

Once you have made your own list, reread it and be shocked at how much shit is on it that is a lot of work to get it all sorted – look at how many different kinds of coloured duct tape you need!!

At some point a feeling of 'it's all too hard right now, I'm so tired' will wash over you. Embrace it. Give up. Go to the fridge, open that nice Sauvignon blanc you were saving, if you're going to die because you didn't have the right colours of duct tape, you might as well do it in the kitchen with a nice glass of wine.[5]

This is where most people get to with prepping and that's ok. Life is already hard enough without having to plan for much harder stuff that probably won't even happen. Just don't complain when it happens because I will totally say I told you so I will come to your house in my I told you so pantsuit and dance around on your verandah singing the I told you so anthem (I won't I will be safely tucked away in my bunker at the First Dog on the Moon Institute – actually I will probably be face down in a compost heap but that's another story.) There is certainly not a bunker at the First Dog on the Moon Institute which is also not in Brunswick Melbourne and no compost heap either.

Let's face it – if civilisation collapses you might prefer to just you know… I mean I'm not advocating that anyone… but a bottle of Nembutal is cheaper, quicker and takes up a lot less space and organisation than enough supplies to last a family of four for six months. True story. Actually that is pretty dark I should probably take that out of the book.[6]

4. SOMETHING YOU WILL NEED

YOUR MOST IMPORTANT TOOL IS… A HEAD LAMP! NOT JUST BECAUSE YOU CAN SEE IN THE DARK WHEREVER YOUR FACE IS FACING BUT BECAUSE WEARING A HEADLAMP SAYS TO PEOPLE – 'I AM NOT TO BE MESSED WITH. I AM WILLING TO LOOK LIKE A DICKHEAD TO GET THE JOB DONE! DO NOT CROSS ME I

HAVE OTHER HEADLAMPS, I HAVE SPARES. NO, YOU CAN'T HAVE ONE'. Other less prepared people will steer clear of you because you look like a maniac especially if you wear it during the day with the light switched off. Don't wear it switched on during the day that is just weird.

Ok you're still here – you must mean business – let's get started on the most important thing.

5. AN EMERGENCY PLAN!

An emergency plan! This is where you get to annoy the other members of your family the most – where will you go, what will you do? Do you know how long it takes to get from your place of work to home? By car? On foote?

Fill out this emergency plan BEFORE an actual emergency don't do it when it is happening or you will probably die.

Make sure everyone in your household understands what they need to do under the various scenarios – frighten any children if you have to otherwise they might not pay attention or why not just agree to leave them behind because they really will slow you down. Then again they might come in handy later as bait or to trade for a chainsaw or a drum of diesel. Who knows you might even end up eating them I am told they taste like chicken.

While you are at it make sure you plan for the scenarios listed in this book plus all the other ones not listed and for any other scenarios that you may not have thought of yet. You cannot be too ready!

'Oh the end of the world came and we were far too well organised so we died horribly,' said nobody ever. Remember to expect the unexpected that tries to kill you – explosion in a thong factory? Underpants or footwear, a tonne of either falling from the sky can be fatal do you have a reinforced underpants-proof roof on your shelter? And just to be extra sure, are you sure you will never ever go outside ever? No you don't. Are you

really ready? (No you are not.) If you live in the country or the bush you will probably have a fire plan – this is just like that except a million times more complicated and with a lot more stuff.

Some of the sorts of things that go into an emergency plan are:-

- Emergency meet up locations in your city where you can meet with family/ team members. If there is a chemical spill or explosion in an underpants factory you might not be able to get home! If you're in the country it doesn't really matter I have been told everyone there just wanders around

wherever they want. I've never been but I hear there is a lot of space and trees and nudity. Plenty of things to hide behind as well. That is something to think about.

— What you will do and/or where you will meet if you are separated/boiled alive in an unexpected tsunami of scalding porcupine urine, how long before you can start to date other people?

— Make sure you have everyone's phone numbers and also this plan printed out and copies given to everyone, plus some maps and even some favourite family recipes (I don't know why but it was on one of those websites and maybe knowing how to make Nan's chocolate pickle gin cake might save your life one day). Get one of those laminating machines and just laminate the absolute shit out of everything they are fantastic.

chocolop
gickle pincake
no
wait....

— Make sure everyone knows where the bug out/bug in/bug off bags locations, documents, equipment and vehicles are/will be depending on their prior location and the nature/duration of the emergency situation. It is that easy.

6. CRITICAL DOCUMENTATION

Good thing you got that laminating machine! Before WETWIPEAWAKI hits get all of your critical documentation in one place: birth certificates, insurance things, passports, family recipes. Whatever, this sounds super boring but stay focused you fool! Not having a laminated photocopy of your passport could kill you apparently. One prepper I read about does a tiny wallet sized version of everything plus two normal sized versions and then laminates them and

puts them in various separate easily accessible secure locations around the place. Easily accessible so that you can grab them in an emergency but also secure because they contain everyone's critical documentation including credit card numbers and you don't just want them lying around for non-preppers to snaffle. Maybe you should leave one at Nan's place as well, and what about a safety deposit box too I mean seriously you have to think of everything it is exhausting. This won't be the first or last time you think to yourself maybe I will just let the plague of robot death fungus have me this is too hard. You are probably right.

Along with your laminated documentation, have laminated photos of your loved ones! That way, if you get separated you can wander the ruined streets of your suburb asking complete strangers if they have seen this handsome slightly shambolic looking cartoonist (just as an example).

7. COMMUNICATIONS

Or more like NO COMMUNICATIONS AT ALL! No TV, no mobile phones, no social media facebook twitter or any of that, there will not be any internet at all. IT IS GOING TO BE FANTASTIC! Seriously though you will need back-up ways to get in touch when the networks all go down do you have access to carrier pigeons? Hang on to them you might need to eat them I am told they taste like chicken. How about two tins and an extremely long piece of string? You could send a postcard actually now that I think about it if the phones are down we're in all sorts of trouble.

Sure there are walkie talkies and CB radios but this is a book for disorganised idiots do you even know where to buy a walkie talkie? Me neither. No if you get separated from your loved ones and they don't turn up at the pre-arranged meeting places (see 5) you are probably on your own. You'll travel lighter without them anyway and between you and me I never really like them. I always thought you could have done better and frankly they didn't treat you as respectfully as you deserve like I have always tried to, and look maybe this is finally the right time for me to tell you... oh here they are now! Awkward. No nothing, it can wait. It's not important I said I don't want to talk about it.

Anyway I'll be fine, I have friends who are vets and they own a vineyard so that is where we are going. There might still be time for you to make friends with vineyard-owning vets, not our ones though, but there must be others. Doesn't even have to be a vet, could be a surgeon with a whisky distillery in an old quarry actually, that sounds way better – we could do a swap. Or I'll just come with you in the first place don't worry I won't tell the vets I never really liked them anyway.

8. PRACTISE YOUR SKILLS! (GET SOME FIRST)

Skills practice is very important because you need to be good at not dying when the SHTF. Learn how to light a fire with dried cat poop and a piece of string then practise, practise, practise!

Do you know how to build a diesel generator? Build one! Quick you have

20 minutes. Build another blindfolded just to make sure you remember. Go and lie down under some shrubs in the park and pretend people going past didn't prepare at all and are now zombies – attack them with a broom handle – but then explain you're just getting ready for the end of the world I'm sure they will understand.

9. OH MY GOD I COMPLETELY FORGOT THE PETS.

Jesus the fucking pets. What do you do with your pets? Do you have a tiny stupid dog? An annoying cat? A huge aquarium full of expensive delicate tropical fish? You idiot – that is such a shit hobby. They need food and carry boxes and probably medicine and stuff. Do you have a friend who is a vet? I used to. There is this bit in The Handmaid's Tale[7] by Margaret Atwood where they are about to flee the regime in the US by pretending they are going to Canada just for the weekend. They don't want anyone to know so they can't take the cat with them, but having a cat hanging around hungry is a bit of a giveaway so he goes out to the shed and kills the cat[8] AND I HAVE BEEN HAUNTED BY THIS SCENE MY WHOLE LIFE.

I have never forgotten it – it is the same reason I don't watch nature documentaries because everyone is always dying horribly – insects are people too you know. There was this David Attenborough one where these killer whales chased a mother grey whale and her calf for hours and hours and the mother fought them and fought them but eventually the calf was too exhausted and just gave up and ALL THE KILLER WHALES DID WAS EAT ITS TONGUE THOSE BASTARDS I did a lot of therapy after that one. I'm not even joking. So if you are thinking that when the TEOTOWELRACK arrives I am going to accidentally kill myself with a whisk or by hitting my head on a bus stop, you are probably right but before that we are going to have to work out what to do with Beyonce, Roy and Chu Chu. All of whom are over ten years old with various stupid medical conditions.

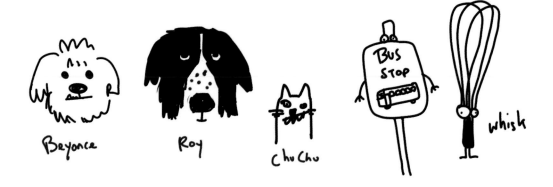

Beyonce   Roy   Chu Chu   Bus Stop   whisk

Where was I?

10. YOU ARE NOT FIT ENOUGH

Something else a lot of preppers focus on is the need to be healthy and fit. Work out and start eating right. Although if all the food disappears suddenly having a few extra kilos might help you last a bit longer unless everyone becomes a cannibal. I am told you taste like chicken. Look it's complicated. In general you will go further survive with less and get fewer illnesses if you are not a portly middle-aged but very handsome soft-handed cartoonist so don't be one of those. Thank goodness I am not. I even have an Akubra (which I bought at the airport, don't judge me).

Does it all sound too hard? Well harden up you big sook you won't last a minute. If you're tired now wait until the Little Sisters of the Unrapturable Home for the Elderly Left Behind over the back fence is suddenly filled with brain-hungry aged zombies! Won't you feel silly when Mrs Poodlington (87) is eating out of your skull with a military-grade spork because you couldn't even get a list finished. I know I will.

Spoooork
/ spoooork

HOW I SURVIVED BEING RAISED BY WOLVES (UNIONISTS) IN THE FOREST (THE SAPPHIRE COAST OF NSW)

Dad's Dad Bob Marlton was an organiser for the Australian Railways Union in Townsville and a member of the ALP for over 50 years. He had lost the toes on his right foot in a shunting incident in Charters Towers in the 30s. Former Prime Minister Paul Keating went to visit Dad's Mum Martha in her retirement village in Townsville after Bob died. We were all pretty pleased with our union and Labor party credentials after that I can tell you. Mum was the union rep for the teacher's federation in the high school in Canberra where she taught for a long time. I have included all this to establish my working-class credentials because the rest of this book is an elitist self-indulgent bourgeois filibuster hahahaha just kidding I am a communist now.

We left Bega for Canberra when I was five and stayed there for the next fifteen years which means I GREW UP IN CANBERRA which should explain PRETTY MUCH EVERYTHING. IT IS WHY I AM LIKE THIS.

Here is an old timey photo of my grandfather's rugby league team from 1920.

If you have ever lived in Canberra you will understand. Great bus stops though. Canberra is great when you are a kiddy – in the 70s it was like a well-lit paddock. I went to 'alternative' high schools because Mum thought I would get the shit beaten out of me if I went to Deakin High and she was right.

I was a hideously lonely child. My two brothers (lovely fellows, Jeremy and Simon) were six and seven years older than me (still are, funnily enough) so I was mostly like an only child. It feels a bit weird writing about this. I had a lovely conversation with Simon just this morning about jonquils which are one of our favourite flowers and he reminded me they grew along the gravel drive near the dairy farm in Gippsland that our other grandad (Jack) used to manage.

I always wanted to be a cartoonist. Actually, I wanted to be an actor, being a cartoonist was my back-up plan. Pretty good back-up plan what could possibly go wrong?

Canberra bus stops which we cruelly laughed at when they arrived and now we are quite fond of them

CHAPTER 3

Bugging in
or bugging out?

Getting this decision wrong (like so many others) in an apocalyptic end of the world situation may kill you.

Bugging in!

Why would you bug in? Why wouldn't you? Sleep in your own bed. Access to fresh towels. Maybe martial law is declared and you can't leave even if you want to. What if it was a typo and marital law is declared your spouse refuses to leave his/her prizewinning chickens. Perhaps your suburb is quarantined because of a virus or hipster plague. Your bug out vehicle is at the bug out mechanics! Roads are blocked. You broke your leg. You can't take your dolphin at short notice. You ignored all of the instructions in this book and didn't plan anything and now there are ubercows from the fifth dimension with acid for blood stampeding up and down the streets.

Bugging in means higher security. You know the layout of your home. You know the good places to hide and where all the weapons are (in the kitchen drawer probably although I think there's a cricket bat in the laundry). If you bug out you are VULNERABLE OUT IN THE OPEN! Also, home is where people who love you will look for you first unless nobody loves you. And you have all your stuff at home, (fresh towels, well-equipped spice rack, pallet of Purity Weasel tinned kidney beans in worcestershire gravy). That junk drawer in the kitchen is going to be more useful than you ever imagined.

Either way, it is time to fortify your home now while there is still a chance. You need to get deadlocks and strengthen your door frames. Learn how to use a trident or nunchucks. Get some watch geese and position them around your home so they make a terrible racket if someone is trying to sneak in. Also I am told they taste like chicken. Windows are terribly insecure, so get rid of these too. Electrify your doormat. Dig a moat (the geese will appreciate it).

Bugging out!

Why would you bug out? You could be ordered to evacuate. Maybe your house has burnt down. It could be infested with chocolate-pickle-gin monsters. Your housemates are massive dickheads and you were moving out anyway leave a passive aggressive note on the fridge.

Should you bug in or out? This decision could mean life or death! Use our handy Ezy2Read Flow Chart to decide!

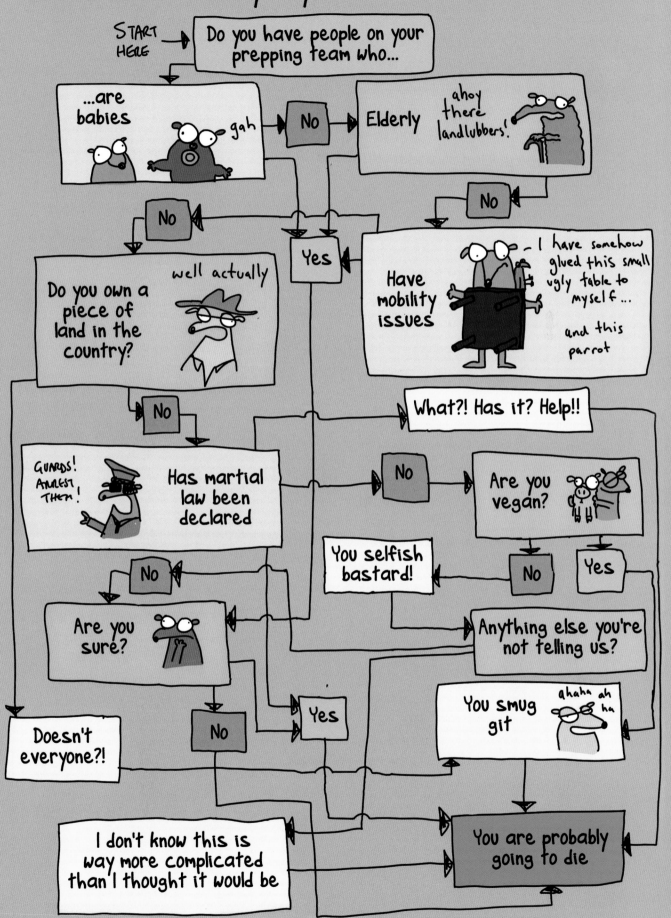

Perhaps you were on twitter bragging about all your prepping supplies and how organised you are and now twitter is coming to kill you and eat all your stuff. Maybe the people who live in the house would like it back 'please let us out of the basement!' it could be any number of things. Whatever, the place you are in is bad and dangerous it is time to go.

BUG OUT LOCATION (BOL) CHECKLIST

So we've figured out that because of a flood/fire/earthquake/tornado/passive aggressive housemate etc you have to get out, but where will you go and how will you get there? When you're a beginning prepper, you probably aren't ready to do a complex bug out route assessment whatever that is, I read it somewhere, but you should have the basics of WHERE you're going to go which includes somewhere to go to. Do you have friends in the country? Are they nice? Perhaps you don't care. They're probably not going to be happy to see you if the world has ended because of a highly contagious disease but this is no time to be fussy. Hardcore preppers go so far as to purchase a piece of land in an isolated location that they can flee to. The super-duper hardcore ones are already living on it, they're off the grid and eating leaves and rocks etc, but we are just beginners and not ready to eat sticks and dirt just yet.

If you don't own a rural hideaway you can just 'scope out' a spot in a national park or similar area. Just make sure no one else is scoping out the same spot. Wouldn't that be funny? How will you know if they are? I haven't the faintest idea, you are on your own with that one. Maybe wait there and see if anyone else comes along and then leap out and show them your bottom.

'I don't want to bug out in that spot Nigel, that person kept on leaping out and showing us their bottom!'

'Good point Mywfanwy we will go somewhere else more bottomless'

Ideally your bug out location will:

- Be one tank of petrol away from home or no more than five days walk if you don't have a car. You should probably get a car though. Although the traffic jams will be terrible. To be really safe you should get a dirt bike as well. And a penny farthing in case the world is attacked by zombie hipsters they are sure to assume you are one of them. And if you are riding a penny farthing you will be you fuckwit.

- Your bug out location should be a long way from highly populated areas. It should be isolated but also accessible from three (3) different routes just in case, you can't be too prepared but also isolated and hard to get to.

- Water, it should have water.

- You should be familiar with it because otherwise you won't know what to expect. What is it like in winter/summer? Is it in an area where there are bushfires or bears? I prefer bears but they will still kill you.

- Is it defendable? Does it have lightning or panthers?

- It should have shelter. Bury a shipping container somewhere on it. Or take a tent. And camping things I suppose too. Unless there is a house on it already. Get a place with buildings on it. Ooh look at you with your fancy house in the country.

– Somewhere to grow food if things get really bad. You'll need a fishing line and the willingness (and tools) to catch furry animals and eat them. It is going to be a lot of hard work luring, enticing, hunting, trapping, squishing, beheading, delifing, boiling and fricasseeing the local wildlife (who apparently taste like chicken fyi). Practise by catching and eating the cats in your neighbourhood. And look out for the Golden Horde.[9]

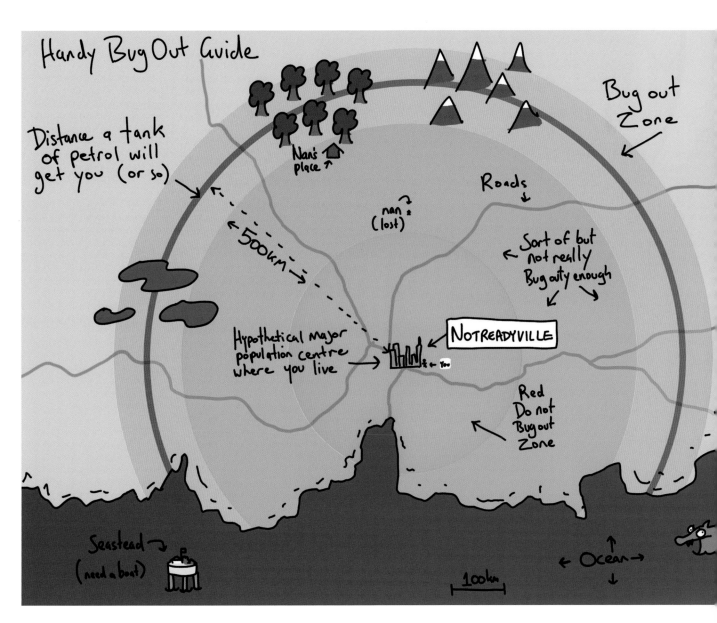

Bug out bag

If you are going to bug out, you will also need a bug out bag. What is a bug out bag? It is a bag you take with you when you bug out, obviously. If you are going to ask stupid questions like that I don't hold out much hope for you.

A bug out bag should be light enough for you to carry great distances but which also contains everything you will ever need to survive forever while civilisation crumbles to dust around you. You will need to do a practise hike with your bag after you have packed it because there is not going to be any point bugging out if you can only get to the end of the street because you took your microwave oven and all your copies of First Dog on the Moon's Cartoon Treasury (which weighs almost a kilo). You will look like an idiot practising with your enormous bag, schlepping your camouflaged military pack up and down the street and is that worth it? Probably not. Maybe wear your headlamp as well and people will just leave you alone. Hardcore preppers have different bug out bags for different situations also an EDC which they take with them everywhere and one in the car as well.

BUG OUT BAG CHECK LIST

1. Sensible shoes (make sure they are an armageddon appropriate colour)
2. Laminated ID
3. Money
4. Chihuahua themed thermos flask
5. Water purifying something
6. Water bottle
7. Fire making something (string and cat poop works apparently)
8. Mirror
9. Flares (the bright light not the trousers)
10. 4 or 5 days' food
11. First aid kit

Bug Out Bag Checklist

12. Actual bag
13. Sanitation supplies
14. Change of underwear
15. A container to cook or boil stuff in
16. Swiss army knife or leatherperson
17. Tactical spork
18. Paracord which is a lightweight nylon kernmantle rope – v handy
19. Phone
20. A torch
21. A lot of guns and/or things for stabbing zombies
22. Gauze
23. Chainsaw
24. Ziplock bags!

10 STEPS TO PACKING OUR BUG OUT BAG!

1. Put in all the stuff you are going to need.
2. But not so much you can't carry it.
3. Have a go at lifting it.
4. Ngggggg
5. Alright that's a bit heavy what can you take out?
6. No you'll need that.
7. And that.
8. A full size coffee machine that runs off a car battery? That is fantastic!
9. Does it heat the milk as well?
10. No no hang on to that the world is ending why be miserable?
11. Fuck it let's drive.

Prepping equipment and supplies

From the First Dog on the Moon Eschatological Institute

Whenever it gets to TERRIYAKIWAKI you'll need all your gear to stand up and do its job first time every time! But which gear is the right gear? Here at the First Dog on the Moon Eschatological Institute we've sourced and tested some of the finest sturdiest most useful post apocalyptic tools for slipping in your bug out bag or that plastic box you keep under the stairs. What do you really need? Let's find out.

1. HOW ABOUT THIS MILITARY GRADE SPORK?

Don't eat with your hands like an animal! This spork like they use in the army[10] has a bottle opener, different sized metric wrench holes, a picking tool for picking, a screwdriver and a handy carabiner. Best of all if you end up at the supermarket fighting over the last dozen tins of Purity Weasel Sustainable Tuna, you can take someone's eye out with it. Certainly handy but you don't need it as much as...

2. THIS 15-IN-1 PARACORD BRACELET! OMG!

A what? A paracord bracelet. It unravels to become 4 metres of incredibly strong lightweight military-grade paracord, that's the stuff used on parachutes to keep you and the parachute connected! Handy! This amazing bracelet has a compass, a thermometer, a whistle, a firestarter, a not very good blade, and a weird screwdriver-wrench thing. You cannot be caught unprepared if you have one of these and yet this is still not the most important thing to have in your bug out bag.

3. PERHAPS IT IS THIS PERSONALISED WATER FILTER!

Stick this in water you're not sure about and suck, it removes 99.99% of bacteria, giardia, cryptosporidium for 1000 litres. That is certainly useful, it might even save your life but you don't need it as much as...

4. THESE FIRST DOG ON THE MOON PLUSH TOYS!

I'm serious. These are real toys that will keep you warm (if you purchase in bulk). Stuff one down your undies and impress people who like folks with bulky undies. These firm but fair toys will frighten away any wolves, they will ward off bad spirits and people who believe in bad spirits because frankly they are a bit scary looking, at least the potato is, look at it! If you're attacked by feral children, you can distract them by throwing a stuffed toy in the other direction. They're jammed full of handy but safe non-flammable stuffing and the bandicoot is posable which means its skeleton is useful wire! True. Seriously though we bought boxes and boxes of these animals a while back and haven't sold as many as we thought that's why they are now only $20 each or a whole set for $80 and available at firstshoponthemoon.com

This is not a joke[11] please buy our plush toys we have to get rid of them we are moving to the country to a remote spot that... no wait I didn't say that. I mean we're not moving but we... need the space to put... erm... an oxygen tent for one of our older rescue dogs! Beyonce has a heart condition and gets winded easily. Actually, that is true too. Look just buy a soft toy and I will stop going on about it.

Sorry, I made it weird. You can buy a tea towel as well if you like.

Handy survival hints to not leave the house without

Here are some things to think about (but not overthink because then you'll be just thinking and not doing anything useful a bit like this sentence is now that it has been going for a while).

Wipe mud over your skin to protect against mosquitoes and people thinking you have had a bath recently.

Don't play the harmonica when polar bears are possibly around because they are attracted to strange noises and terrible music. Try a travel glockenspiel instead.

Use a corn chip to hold a flame the way a candle wick does except it is a corn chip. I have not tried this and it sounds like bullshit but if I'm desperate enough I won't have any qualms about setting fire to a whole bunch of corn chips. I am born to survive!

Use a potato peeler on thin branches to create very curly wood shavings which can be used to turn very small flames into big ones or to make a hilarious comedy beard for those cold winter nights.

Always check your boots for funnel webs whether the world is ending or not those bastards.

Briefs or boxers – do you want your sherrins graciously contained or wandering about your dacks like a couple of wildebeest doing a walk of shame?

At night IT IS DARK! Seriously! If you go outside now and you don't live in the country you can see because there are lights around the place. I know it sounds ridiculous but it is true.

Learn to odourless cook – chances are it won't taste amazing but you also won't attract hungry people or leopards. Boiling stuff in a zip-lock bag is probably the simplest and most humiliating way to do this.

Go out and get some oxygen absorbers, mylar bags, whole powdered eggs, freeze-dried sausage crumbles, milk powder, cheese in a bag, butter in a can, potato flour, seafood extender, rice, pasta in a hessian sack, dried piffle, dried fruit, lonely fruit, tins in a big wooden box, chocolate, whisky in a bag and frozen peas. You won't need any of these things but it is good to practice buying things that make people look at you funny.

You will probably need to defend yourself at some point so you should read a book about self defence or maybe practise hitting things with a stick, you could even sharpen one end of it or buy a gun. Do you have access to a spacecraft?

Carry a big stick and be a gun

TRUE LIFE SURVIVAL STORIES III

HOW I SURVIVED BEING RAISED BY FEMINIST WOLVES

Mum was a feminist ratbag in the 70s and so were most of her friends from what I recall. It was an interesting time. I read the *Female Eunuch* when I was 14 – I don't think I understood a word of it but FEMINISM! I WAS TOO! Seriously it was good for me. Made me the man I am today and I am a National Treasure.[12]

When I was a teen I volunteered (and later worked) at a community radio station (2XX). I think I played a lot of hard-core punk music and as much Ramones as possible. It was rather jolly fun. 2XX was full to the brim with lesbians and communists (and a lot of people who were really, really into folk music now that I recall) and I learned that the personal is political which is quite a complicated notion for a troubled teen. It was wall-to-wall reel-to-reel tape decks and even some dreadful radio comedy which was the prelude to the dreadful radio comedy I have been inflicting on people over the last few years. Didn't we have a lovely time. At 2XX I was radicalised online and they didn't even have the internet then. Does anyone remember when we didn't have the internet and we lived like wild animals under a bush? Seriously though, for years I felt guilty that I was a bloke and I was white (mostly that I was a bloke though). I agonised. I agonised over it. But then I got over it and moved on (although you can never really leave). I always thought that one is not much use to the revolution if one is banging on about the oppression of one's non-oppression. Indeed, one is not. You may think that is wrong, but

what are you going to do, argue with a book? Don't make it weird with you sitting on a train shouting at a book you're oppressing the other commuters.

I'm not saying white men don't have lots of feelings, we totally do, we are also victims of capitalism and the world being bad. In some ways we have more to lose and less to gain if you want to look at it from a self-indulgent perspective, but that is not even an argument worth having unless you are trying to work out how to stop it from changing. I have loads of white man feelings all the time, but they're not a solid foundation for a political analysis (ping Sky News at Night). (Actually for me it is an excellent foundation, but I am special, this is my gift and my burden, would you like to buy a tea towel?)I learnt a lot about politics and justice and the way the world could be from my mum and my dad. But I have also had to do a great deal of therapy.

I was bitten by a bee once.

PART II
THE APOCOLI

ARMAGEDDON EXPLAINED

Exciting! We lurch now into the eschatological[13] intestines of our journey. How exactly is the world going to end? So many possibilities, and here we list some but not all of them because who knows?

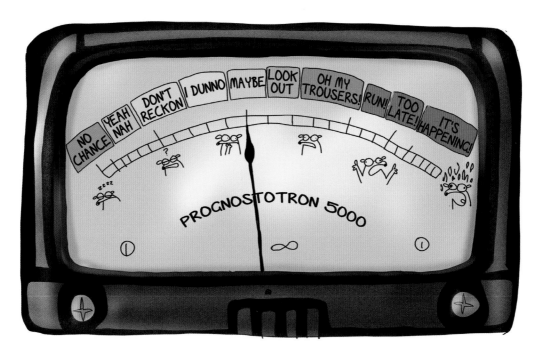

Our motto here at the Institute is 'Be the readiest you can be and if you can't be ready, be fast.'[14]

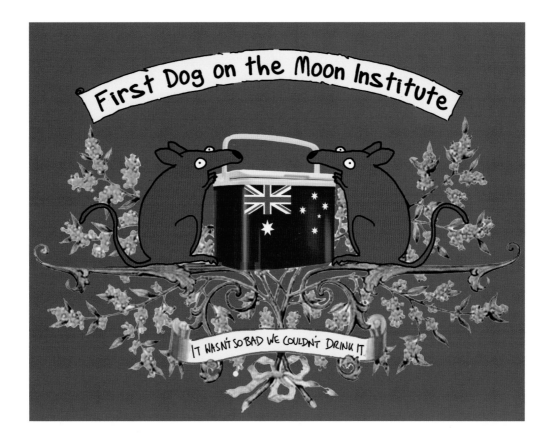

Did you know that the Earth has experienced five mass extinctions before this one and the one that we may or may not shortly be having? Every 90 million years or so the planet chucks a wobbly and gets rid of most of the life on itself, spends a couple of million years just having some me time then starts again. Hopefully this isn't a complete extinction event because even this book won't help if everyone isn't here.

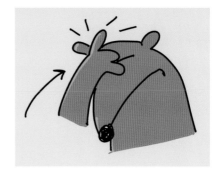

What follows are the most likely apocali – as determined by our panel of professional apocalologists and eschatologers (all completely supported by Internet Science). You will learn how to avoid and/or deal with them or whether you should simply lie down and let them roll over you to experience the sweet release of death. We helpfully quantify each apocali by various factors which we feed into the Prognostotron which uses our patented Guesstimalgorithm Engine to come up with a likelihood quotient so you can get a vague sense of which apocali is more likely to happen within a time frame that will inconvenience and/or kill you but without enough confidence to be able to plan for it specifically. You're welcome.

At the First Dog on the Moon Eschatological Institute these science potoroos are analysing results from our state of the art apocali prediction instrument The Prognostotron 5000

CHAPTER 4

Bees!

What if it is BEES?! Not an attack from bees, although that would be terrible, what if all the bees disappeared? There won't be anymore honey for one thing but also… THE BEEPOCALYPSE.

What is it?

How good are bees? So good! Critical to the world's ecosystems. Of the 100 crop species that provide 90 percent of the world's food supply, over 70 are pollinated by bees. At least it is something like that many. Did you know that[15] there are something like 20,000 species of bees on Earth and they are only the ones we know about.

There was this one bee scientist that said there are up to fifty trillion bees give or take a few. Fifty trillion bees! That is a lot of bees – if you put all those bees end to end you would be stung to death in no time at all and it would serve you right.

Bee

Bee Scientist

Aside from the stinging I am completely pro-bee. In Tasmania they have these huge bumblebees (*Bombus terrestris*) like big fat flying furry gnocchi – fantastic creatures apparently they are introduced though and are bad for the native bees. Bad bees. I would totally watch that movie. Anyway you wouldn't want a family of them moving in next door even though being bad bees is their job. I do not think you can reason with a bee. Certainly not a big bad bee. Did you know that the male bee's penis explodes during sex? There is a lot to unpack here.

Death Gnocci

All around the world bee colonies are collapsing and we don't really know why. Bee scientists (wouldn't that be a good job – imagine having a business card that said 'Bee Scientist' on it) know a bit about what is causing the bees to disappear, they have a lot of bee theories, but they don't know enough to stop it.

What will happen?

If the bees all die, half of all the food stuff at the supermarket will disappear including but not limited to coffee, almonds, apples, avocados, cashews, blueberries, grapes, peaches, capsicum, strawberries, walnuts, watermelons. WATERMELONS! COFFEE! ALSO COTTON NO MORE COTTON UNDERPANTS! That change of underwear in your bug out bag may just be the last undies on Earth.

If you ask a prepper they will say COTTON KILLS! Why? If it is cool and your cotton shirt/pants/undies get wet they stay wet for a long time. Cotton is great in summer but in cold weather it is bad. Cotton is great at absorbing and holding water which drops your body temperature five times faster than air. Before you know it you have hypothermia and you have died. Imagine the world is ending because of an asteroid impact but you die because your undies froze your whatsit to death. An embarrassing and unnecessary tragedy. Don't be the frozen whatsit person. Something to think about.

Post-bee we will still have wheat, corn, rice and soybeans as they don't need pollination. Potatoes, tomatoes, and carrots only need a tiny bit of help from bees so we might be able to pollinate them ourselves. Dressed as bees! Yes please. Also, pigs and chickens don't need pollinated food. But pigs and chickens are quite nice people and if we are going to save the world we will need to stop eating them anyway.

I certainly should. A diet of just pork crackling with chicken salt and potatoes the world will die of scurvy.

So we won't all starve to death EXCEPT that in the process of changing the Earth's agricultural production over to these non-pollen-requiring foods it is pretty likely the world's economy will collapse. It will be bad. Now we really are talking apocalypse! Food riots! Martial law! War! Bumblebees!

Tell your children there will never be delicious breakfast cereal ever again because the baby boomers murdered all the bees.

What is the likelihood?

What is the chance of the world's economy collapsing because all the bees die? Good question. If we were working furiously all around the globe to reduce the use of pesticides and figure out what was happening with the bees and how to mitigate climate change, then I reckon we could say

yeah nah

...but we're not, so it's more of a

We really don't know a) what we are doing to the bees b) how exactly we are doing it (pesticides, habitat, reality television) or c) what will happen if/when they all cark it. Global economic collapse is just one of the grim options.

There would still be figs though, because did you know figs are pollinated by a tiny wasp that climbs into the fig's ostiole (fig hole) lays eggs and DIES. EVERY FIG CONTAINS A DEAD WASP. ALSO WASP SEX! True story. Maybe we don't want to live in this world. Get a fig wasp up your ostiole! (See cartoon about *Vespa mandarinia* on page 77)

How to prepare

With a global economic collapse you will probably see it coming though it might be quick. Food shortages and so on won't be instantaneous. This will give you time to bug out to your rural hideaway where you can grow food and a pig (just so you have a friend, bugging out can be lonely).

Your new friend

You will need to bug out because wait for it we are out of bugs! Ahahah – bees – get it you see bees are bugs and anyway that was a bug out joke it took me ages to come up with that.

Food supplies will be critical obviously, so take food and also you will need seeds of plants that do not require pollination! And these will be harder to source once it is clear that the bees are going, so as with everything else in this book GET IN EARLY TO GET YOUR BEE-PROOF SEEDS OR STARVE.

Water and power won't initially be interrupted so you will have to sort your shit out. But you won't be able to stay in the city. Or eat honey ever again. Say hi to your pig for me.

The International Society for Cartoons about Global Warming and Giant Insects proudly presents:

Another Cartoon about Global Warming and Giant Insects

This week – The Giant Hornet (Vespa mandarinia) wants to kill you

The latest Intergovernmental Panel on Climate Change report is out. It says a whole bunch of stuff. The gist of it is that 97% of scientists agree with the other 97% of scientists that...

WE ARE ALL GOING TO DIE!

Don't make me say it again. Because I will. Over and over.

All the other scientists (3%) probably tuck their shirts into their underpants. They look like this and go on Alan Jones' radio program where they say things about Climate Science like:

It's a farce and it's a circus!

But that's not important right now, what is important is that as a result of record breaking heat waves GIANT HORNETS HAVE KILLED 28 PEOPLE IN CHINA

I WARNED YOU PEOPLE ABOUT GIANT INSECTS IT IS AS IF YOU AREN'T LISTENING TO ME

GIANT MOTHERFUCKING HORNETS!!!

5 FUCKING CENTIMETRES!!

The IPCC report doesn't mention Giant Hornets at all! I checked. I downloaded the pdf and did a word search for "giant hornet" just as if I WAS A SCIENTIST! I did science to it!

IPCC REPORT.pdf (page 1 of 2,216)
Search: GIANT MOTHERFUCKING HORNETS!!!
Found on 0 pages   Done

WHY ARE THE IPCC HIDING THE GIANT HORNET TRUTH?!

Vespa mandarinia are 5cm long and their venom contains an enzyme that can dissolve human tissue, too much of it can bring renal failure and death.

Their swarms can travel up to 40km an hour and sting people up to 200 times. The sting feels like "a hot nail".

These hornets are the greatest moral challenge of our time. They are headed for Europe and the USA. Eventually they must come here! And what if they come here...

ON BOATS!

OH MY GOD IT IS THE PERFECT STORM! IT WILL BE UNBEARABLE.

I don't think I can take it any more

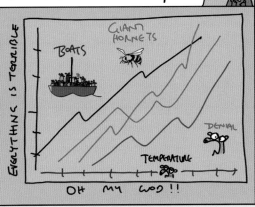

CHAPTER 5

Influenzageddon

What is it?

Imagine a huge global plague! It is easier to organise than you might think, here is how to cook a virus!

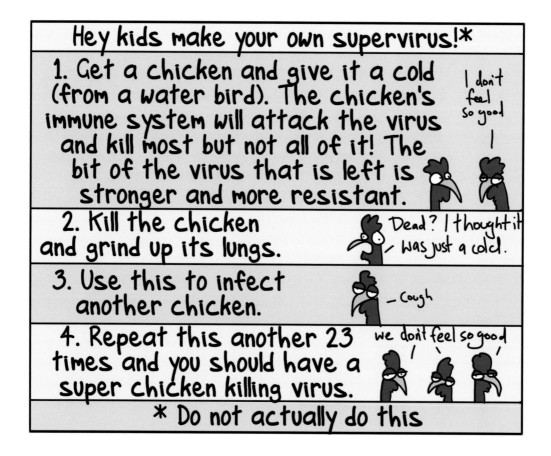

How does one survive a planet wide megaflu? Perhaps one does not.

Some factory animals live in their faeces for their entire lives. A small teaspoon of infected chicken poop can hold enough virus to infect hundreds of chickens. But why would you put infected chicken poop in a teaspoon? Because you're the sort of person that gives chickens a cold and then grinds up their lungs that is why. You pervert.

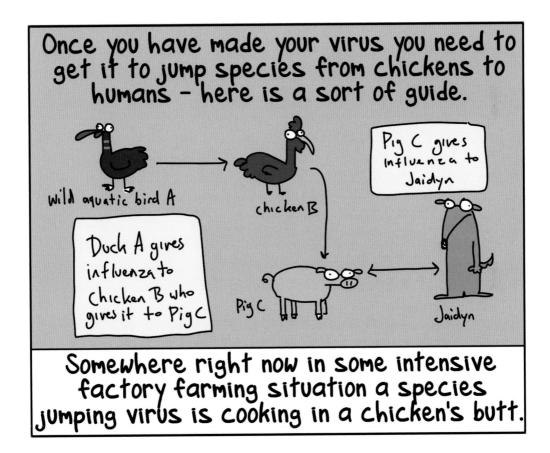

There have been many outbreaks of swine and bird flu over the years, we're just waiting for one that moves faster, kills quicker and is more resistant to really jump the species barrier and then we'll all be in a Gwyneth Paltrow movie faster than you can say I don't want to be in a Gwyneth Paltrow movie. Disease!

Unless you are a doctor you are screwed on this one regardless of whether or not you are estranged from Dustin Hoffman. Don't be Gwyneth Paltrow be Dustin Hoffman catching the tiny monkey! I love plague movies they are almost as good as tidal wave movies.

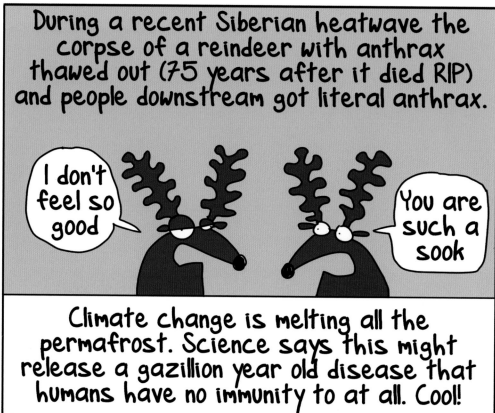

There are diseases you haven't even heard of that could kill you on the bus tomorrow. Some of them will be turning up thanks to climate change which will cause warmer temperatures that big diseases like malaria, cholera and dengue fever are fond of, as well as global shifts in the behaviour and numbers (HUGE INCREASES) of various animals and insects like flies and mosquitos, but also there are ancient diseases hidden in the ice which are being released. It happened in Siberia it could happen in Bungendore.

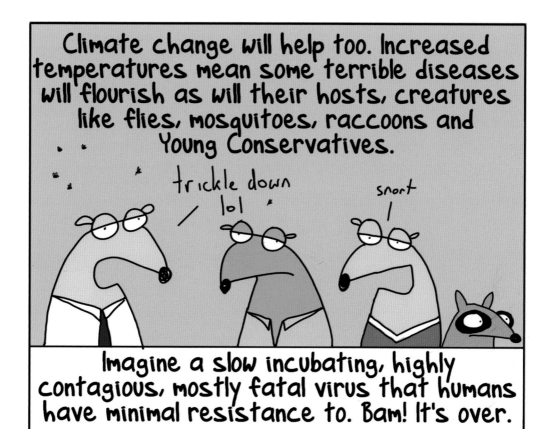

What will happen?

If there was a global disease outbreak, all of the hospitals would be overwhelmed, martial law would be declared and Dustin Hoffman would have to try to stop Donald Sutherland from firebombing your town because they found the tiny monkey and developed a vaccine. Donald don't do it! Stand down soldier! But will they do it in time? Not if you are Gwyneth Paltrow.

You might bug in – but you would really have to stay in for the duration of the disease which could be months. Don't answer the door. Seriously.

Or, if you were going to bug out, and the roads weren't blocked and so on, you would have to get to your BOL and stay there and then really really bug in. It depends on how fast the disease moves and what the official response to it is. Have you practised your emergency evacuation plan over and over like a weirdy loser? Have you? Last year in Melbourne, we had an 'asthma storm event' an unlikely (but well-documented) incident in which strong winds blew huge quantities of rye grass pollen over the city. This pollen is normally too big to get into people's snouts, but an enormous thunderstorm caused the pollen to go rapidly from being a few largish parts per million in the air to a gazillion teeny parts per million. Suddenly, people who had never experienced asthma were struggling to breathe, ambulances and emergency wards were overwhelmed thirteen people died it was really terrible and quite scary – no one knew what was going on. While the authorities knew it was a slim possibility, they were completely unprepared for it. The storm itself only lasted an evening but the complications lasted for weeks for some people.

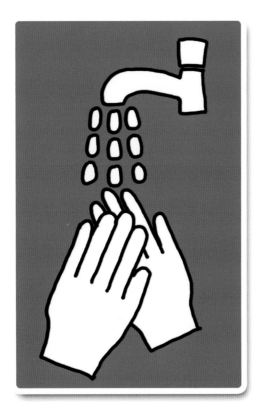

And we haven't even mentioned bioterrorism yet or biotechnology. What if ISIS were cooking up something deliberately and released it? I am sure they'd be happy for the world to end. Or Nazis! That is just the sort of thing Nazis would do. ISIS and the Nazis are probably working on it together right now.

What is the likelihood?

Actually, this particular apocali is the most likely of all the apocalypses. It has happened many times in the past and civilisation is not only not set up to handle it, we are in fact set up really well to make it way more terrible. Air travel, capitalism, tights as pants will all make a global pandemic much worse.

Imagine you are travelling, you get your boarding pass on your phone then, when you are getting on the plane, you hand your phone to the hostie and they scan it and hand it back to you. Not just your phone that you never clean, which is full of warm little holes and which you put next to your mouth, but the phone of every person on the plane and then they touch your phone, all those people going to and from other cities and countries. There was this one study that said smartphones have more bacteria than AN ACTUAL PUBLIC TOILET!

VICTOR

GERMS

lol I know right!?

MASSIVE DISEASE VECTOR VICTOR

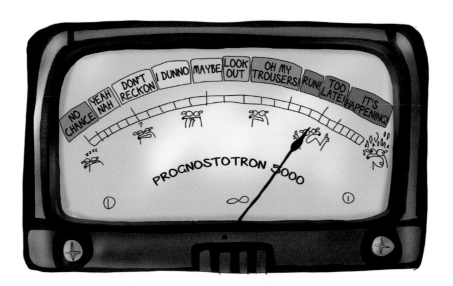

How to prepare and what to do also panic now

Don't expect that the hospital or medical services will be able to help you with a proper global pandemic. The idea is to not have contact with people or things or water that you haven't filtered yourself.

Here is a list of stuff you will need (along with the other stuff in the other lists you will also need – make sure your list of lists is up to date). You'll probably need to isolate yourself at home for eight to twelve weeks at a minimum or so, to really let the disease kill everyone else except you. The key thing about everything on this list is that as it says in the cartoon and I cannot stress this enough YOU HAVE TO HAVE EVERYTHING YOU NEED ALREADY AT HOME! YOU CANNOT LEAVE THE HOUSE ONCE THE PLAGUE ARRIVES!

YOU WILL NEED:

- Water and food obviously. Enough for however many people you have for twelve weeks.
- Vaccine for whatever the disease is that is ravaging the global population. (This can be quite tricky to organise. Are you a doctor? Do you know any vets?)
- 15 litres of liquid bleach per person.
- 4 boxes of those weird plastic doctor gloves per person.
- Goggles and face shields.
- N95 masks – (the 95 stands for filters out 95% of particles and hopefully the other five per cent aren't the poisonous ones).
- Antibacterial soap or hand wipes for meticulous hand washing – a lot of hand washing.
- Dummies' guide to really thorough hand washing (laminated obviously).
- 100 metre roll of clear 4 mil plastic sheeting for setting up an isolation room or maybe you want to be a serial killer like Dexter.
- Duct tape (Duck Tape) – for setting up an isolation room (or repairing your duck).
- Enough HEPA filters for every window in the house.
- 50 kg of lime per person – for provisional toilets.
- 50 kg of limes per person for gin and tonic you are going to need a drink.
- 50 heavy-duty black super-duper garbage bags per person – for provisional toilets and garbage. And get some extra ones, because who doesn't like a good garbage bag. I know I do.

- 50 kilos of kitty litter per person – for sick people's body fluids clean up. How gross is this? When I set out to write this book I didn't think I'd be recommending that people buy commercial quantities of kitty litter even if they don't have an enormous cat.
- 100 rolls of toilet paper per person.
- 20 rolls of paper towels per person.
- Strong dishwashing soap.
- Water-filtration gear.
- Water-collection, storage and carrying containers – get a waterbob![16] I'm serious it is a thing.
- Safety goggles and/or a face shield will help protect the eyes (potential point of infection).
- Disposable coverall suits for the whole family.
- Shovel, axe and a chainsaw (mainly for getting rid of zombies).
- I even watched a video about how to remove contaminated gloves.
- Or you could just kill yourself seriously what a kerfuffle.

CHAPTER 6

Electromagnetic pulse in my pants

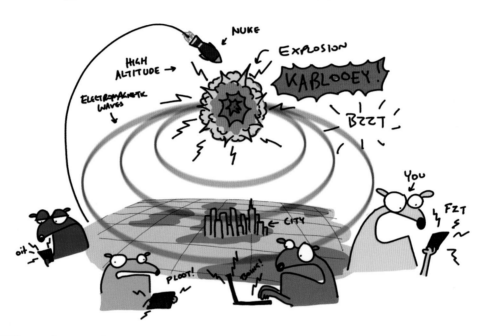

What is it?

Imagine all the electricity disappearing! Ok it is invisible anyway but what if all the devices that need it stopped getting it. Also cars didn't work any more. That is what an electromagnetic pulse does. It is like a tsunami of electromagnet energy that blasts all your electrical equipment and stops the parts that makes it go (this might be a bit technical for some people) by causing a voltage surge in the wiring or something.

A large enough electromagnetic pulse can totally ruin everyone's day by fritzing all the electrical doohickeys and other useful things in a huge area like a whole country. A big enough EMP over your city or general location could end up knocking out the power for days or even weeks PERHAPS FOREVER! It would ruin the phone system and the internet which would be great until people started dying. Hospitals, public transport, refrigerators containing delicious ice-cold beer, all would be rendered inert by this fiendish occurrence.

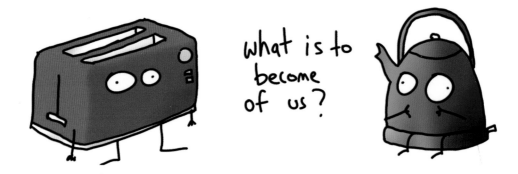

There are number of different ways this alleged EMP could happen. Your common or garden high altitude electromagnetic pulse (HEMP) is the result of a nuclear detonation just inside the stratosphere using a missile or perhaps one of those excellent balloons that goes into space. The other option is that our dear friend the actual Sun could have coronal mass ejection causing a geomagnetic storm resulting in a solar electromagnetic pulse (SEMP) and haven't we all had one of those in the bath. A huge SEMP happened in 1859, but electricity wasn't invented then so nobody minded. In 1989 solar carrying-on shut down the Hydro-Quebec power grid and ruined all the poutine. There are other ways of doing an EMP but only nerds care about those all you need to know is that there is no more television and your filthy bacteria-covered iPhone is metaphorical poop now as well.

What will happen?

EMP scientists say it will inflict a monstrous blackout so terrible that not even your brick-like Kmart clock radio will survive it. Planes might not fall out of the sky but the air traffic control towers would all go down. Just fyi.

What is the likelihood?

What is the likelihood of this beer ruining event taking place? Well that depends on many things, countries like China and Russia and the United States certainly have the capacity to do it but it would be bad for business. The Sun could do it – one bit of the internet says there is a twelve per cent chance it will happen in the next ten years! That is a bit of a lottery like the rest of the universe so idk. EMPs get preppers very excited because it is the sort of thing Iran or North Korea or the United Nations would do if they could just get their hands on the gear and perhaps they are building it right now. We are giving this one a yeah nah.

How to prepare

Get a Faraday cage! This apparently reduces the likelihood of your electrics fritzing – your freezer is a faraday cage did you know that? I work at the *Guardian* and I am not even shitting you, sometimes I have to put my iPhone in the freezer because we are talking about secret stuff. Paranoid? Absolutely, but it is rather fun. The best thing to do is store all of your important

Faraday
(free range)

electrical equipment in your freezer just in case. Here is a fun fact: a HEMP caused by a nuclear bomb will probably ruin all the cars but a SEMP caused by a solar storm won't. Go figure. You will need to know which sort of EMP it is before you decided to bug in or bug out. (This is because if the cars aren't working, the roads will be full of stationary cars, whereas if the cars are working the roads will be full of stationary cars). Anyway. Is it a SEMP (solar electromagnetic pulse) a HEMP ('High' altitude electromagnetic pulse) or perhaps a HUMP (electromagnetic pulse caused by too many camels)?

What should you actually do?

This one is tricky – it is instantaneous so bugging in is going to be the safest option initially – also your BOV might not be working. And the roads will be terrible. But after a few days things will get really unpleasant as there won't be any running water and looting will have cleared out the supermarkets. All the fire/police/hospital/power station people will go home to look after their families because everything will be turning to fertiliser.

You will need torches and batteries and so on – these should be unaffected by the EMP but you should have one of those annoying hand powered torches that don't really work anyway. And all of the other stuff you need look I can't be bothered making another list you have made it this far you make one here I've put in some empty space.

Things I need if there is a HEMP, SEMP or HUMP.

1. Camel trap
2. Bad torch
3. Tactical spork
4. Bumwizzle
5.
6.
7.
8.
9.
10.
11.
12.
13.
14.
15.
16.
17.
18.
19.
20.

HOW I SURVIVED BEING A NOT VERY GOOD ROCK PROMOTER AND ALSO NOT VERY GOOD AT A FEW OTHER JOBS AS WELL

I worked in the rock promotions department at that community radio station I was talking about earlier. It was not as good as it sounds but it was still quite good.

This one time I accidentally helped the roadie for The Stranglers steal a slab of Melbourne Bitter from a fridge at the uni bar in Canberra – remember the uni bar!? I do! Good times. Anyway, helping that guy steal beer was a slightly terrifying act of unintentional gormlessness but I hope Dave Greenwood (the greatest keyboard player in the history of popular music) drank one of those beers. I thought The Stranglers were the scariest band of them all.

I remember a time in my 20s when all I really wanted was $2 to buy a cup of coffee and to write a cheque[17] for the phone bill that wouldn't bounce.

CENTRELINK WILL NOT REST UNTIL IT HAS STRIPPED THE LAST SCRAP OF FLESH FROM YOUR BONES

When I was on the dole, which was at various times for five or six years in the 80s, I learnt a series of extremely painful but useful lessons about bureaucracies and governments and the difference between what is said by the people who run things and the reality of everyone else's lived lives.

Not being able to get a job when you want one is extremely shit. Then when you add the idiot cycle of attending the unemployment office to be interviewed about why you don't have a job, are you looking for a job and we will help you get a job (they will not help you to get a job) it is a depressing, dehumanising grind. The best thing about getting a job was no longer having to deal with Centrelink (it was the C.E.S. back then).

The real purpose of welfare seems to be to deter people from using welfare, I am grateful literally every day that I no longer need it and I am delighted that the money I pay to the government goes to support someone who can't or won't 'just go out and get a job'. My great and good wishes go to the people who take my hard-earned dollars and buy junk food, alcohol, cigarettes and illegal drugs it is none of my fucking business what you do with that money. I am incapable of making consistently good choices in my life so why should they have to? Go well and all power to you.

I got to be a young man living a normal depressing life that was probably a lot better than it felt. It is not that youth is wasted on the young – that is stupid – it is just that all that time spent worrying about stuff could be spent not worrying about stuff. Actually it is still like that now what am I talking about?

I worked as a pizza delivery person and I delivered telegrams for a while, remember telegrams?! They came out of a machine (not even a fax!) and you put them in an envelope and rode your postie bike to someone's house. Two-hour turn around time. Seems like the Flintstones now. I also worked as a waiter which I am very bad at. I moved to Sydney, where I didn't become an actor or cartoonist like I planned, I moved to Philadelphia for a while, the USA was like being on TV except people could actually shoot you. Unlike some people, I got to be a young man and despite my best efforts I did not die. Then Sydney again I went to art school but didn't finish you would never have guessed. Then Melbourne which is where this book is being written. At some point after my delightful daughter was born I became a call centre person and worked my way up to being a call-centre manager. A well-run call centre is a beautiful thing, call centre-enthusiasts will understand. But they can also be brutal life-sapping hell holes.

Where possible I tried for the former, but corporate Australia is not an environment that encourages that sort of thing, it is not conducive to being anything other than a complete arse. I tried to apply what I knew about social justice and niceness, along with my naturally generous personality to all my various activities and jobs and you will be shocked to learn I experienced limited success. I think I got retrenched two or three times. All the while I was working as a freelancer, freelance cartooning is not a life it is a punishment.

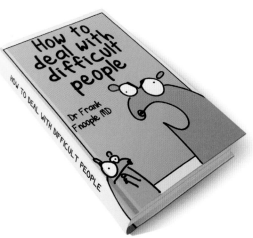

CHAPTER 7

The apocalyptic incarceration of Eaten Fish

(he is not yet dead they have tried to kill him but he will not give up)

Here is a story about a small apocalypse (small unless it is happening to you).

I am sitting in my studio – a small concrete chamber among many others in an artisanal inner-city warehouse. It is dusty and noisy but also cheap and the light pours in through the graffiti-covered plate-glass window. The bike path runs right past, the train line is just beyond that, so I get to pretend I am a gritty and arty artist, almost like a real one as I drink my takeaway flat white and glare at the easel or the Wacom or the pages of this book – bikes and trains rattle past all day, I love it.

I rented the studio to paint – but it became the cartoon studio as well. Home at the First Dog on the Moon Institute, there is room to paint but I have terrible discipline. The Institute is full of wonderful and busy-making distractions. One example among many, are the numerous dogs and cat who have opinions about things and come in and out all day to explain their passions, so I rented a studio (was told, 'go and rent a studio!') ostensibly to paint but knowing I had to write this book as well. I am trying to paint 'light falling on things' and am unfailingly terrible.

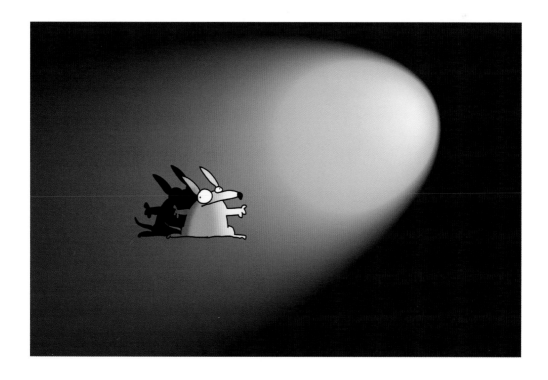

That of course is the point of practising. And there are moments when I can see glimpses of what it might look like in some imagined future when I feel like I know what I am doing.

'I will sit and paint and listen to the trains and the bicycles, and then I will write and listen to the trains and the bicycles.'

And while I am painting or writing or more likely faffing about on the internet, Ali comes on to one of our chat apps – he is telling me what it is like to be on a hunger strike – he told me he was starting one the other day.

Ali is a young Iranian man – a cartoonist – I know some of his back story but I also try not to know unless he tells me directly. These are genuinely dangerous times (mainly for him but who knows these days). Our government acts with brutal impunity and complete disregard for human rights. I feel it is safer for him if he is not telling his story unless he needs to.

In all seriousness, it feels like some kind of cold war (of course I have never been in one) and things are on a need to-know basis. I have been speaking to Ali for a couple of years now – very occasionally on the phone, mostly on various messaging apps. It started when I received an email one day from my now dear friend Janet who asked, 'Would you be interested in mentoring a young asylum seeker who is a cartoonist, he is currently detained on Manus Island'. I said sure, and off we went. At various points along the way, with people campaigning for his (and others' release)

he won an international cartooning award for bravery. He won a human rights award which I tearfully accepted on his behalf at a fancy dinner :(
He is one of the higher profile detainees, which I think helps sometimes but also makes life far more difficult for him. A camp like Manus is not the sort of place you want to get a lot of attention.

In the beginning of our friendship I didn't know what to say to Ali – how do you talk to a guy who has been detained in a concentration camp for years, is routinely suicidal and has various other complex and cruel mental health problems that he is not receiving treatment for? They don't teach this in cartoon school. Actually, they don't teach anything useful in cartoon school, it is a rubbish place, which is why I didn't go.

I figured out pretty quickly that it didn't matter how I felt about it – it just needed to be done – we talked about cartoons a lot in the beginning – he was

excited because I was a 'famous' cartoonist and he was... I don't know... stuck in a tropical gulag bored out of his mind while worrying if he was going to be murdered or assaulted every day.

We talked a lot about what the camp was like (it was extremely boring and filthy and brutal thanks to the guards and the other detainees). Ali has OCD and various other conditions and is hugely anxious a lot of the time. He has panic attacks and scrubs himself until he bleeds, he gets little or no medication for these things.

Even so, I have noticed he has gotten stronger I don't know how – he isn't the same young man I started talking to – winning the cartoon award meant a lot, but also nothing – getting published and getting a website and acclaim for his cartoons meant a lot but also nothing while he remains in there. He can't go home he assures me they will execute him if he is refouled and I have no reason to believe that they won't. Sounds like a pretty standard procedure for the Iranian government from what I hear. He just has to try to live through assaults by the PNG police and the other asylum seekers. At the time of writing, he is in an isolation compound to protect him from assault by other asylum seekers, but the guards regularly threaten to move him back into the regular population.

And poor me I have had to deal with my powerlessness and my impotent fury and what is my country doing? I didn't vote for this government but so what?

I try really hard not to tell Ali what to do – I mean all my ideas and opinions are fantastic and my useful advice is always right, but what do I actually know about anything? What do I know about living in the Manus camp for four years? I told him I understood why he was on a hunger strike, but I didn't want him to die – that I loved him, lots of people love him – I think he knows this – and maybe that is why he is still alive, I don't know. He is very suicidal these days, but they watch them closely. Border Force really don't care what happens to them as long as they don't die because it looks bad. Because the minister will be pressured to answer questions about it, questions he won't answer because he is a liar and the worst person on Earth. I think the hunger strike gave Ali some agency.

He weighs fifty kilos – I can't imagine what that is like in an adult man – I mean, I weigh more than two Ali's (I am currently in between my thin phases – have been for a while now).

I google 'hunger strikes' and try to figure out what might happen. I'm not a counsellor or a health care professional. They don't teach hunger strikes in cartoon school either.

RUF-115.   Ali-Dorani

I said:

**Christ man what are they saying
to you do they even know?**

> **Yes IHMS* comes and check me**

What do they say?

> **They say I have to eat**

Well they would say that yes

And then he posts a gif of that sloth from *Ice Age* being stunned and falling backwards with its feet in the air – he is saying 'der!'.

---

* The health service contracted by the Australian government.

And it is hilarious – this fucking guy – he is starving to death and posting gifs.

**For a fifty-kilo guy on a hunger
strike you are pretty funny**

Yes, it is funny.

**I can't tell you what to do, but I don't want
you to die – eat a sandwich, you dickhead.**

I ask him what the plan is, maybe something he would have talked to Janet about – (who should be made Australian of the year, FYI).

Are we going to the media?

**I'll be close to die after forty-six kilos. I have no fat and energy
or muscles so after a few days my liver can't find energy and
fat and starts taking fat from brain and other important parts.**

Lots of people face death and brutality every day – and I am writing this in a painting studio in an artisanal warehouse in Brunswick I have a lot of feelings. And I am sitting here talking to this talented lively young man who is probably going to die soon. I would have been dead for two years by now if they locked me in Manus.

Update – Ali didn't die. He stopped after nineteen days. He also didn't receive any post-hunger strike treatment even though that can be an equally dangerous time because of the complications of starving for so long then eating again. Those brutal fuckers. Six months later at the time of finally sending this to the printers, Ali has been moved to Port Moresby. The Australian Government is forcibly closing the Manus camp and evicting everyone. Everyone must go to Lorengau or be homeless, both of which are even more dangerous than the Manus camp. We are not sure what the plan for Ali is. He won't last a week outside the Manus camp.

What is it?

A detention regime in which the government detains people seeking asylum (who they describe as 'illegal maritime arrivals') indefinitely in two camps, one on Manus Island in Papua New Guinea and one on Nauru.

This regime is in contravention of various international treaties on human rights and has been widely condemned as cruel, barbaric and dangerous. It has also been widely praised by conservative xenophobic governments around the world and has given them an immoral license to behave in a similar way.

What will happen?

The people on Manus and Nauru have been there for four years. Some have died in different circumstances and the rest suffer from varying degrees of mental health problems, illness and so on. They are occasionally refouled and bullied into returning back to the countries they fled. The Australian government has created 2000 people who will haunt the Earth like broken ghosts until they die.

What is the likelihood?

We never thought it could happen in this country. Although, considering Australia's history and a whole lot of the things that have already happened in this country, we probably shouldn't have been so surprised now that I think about it.

And here we are. Something about how this is a gateway drug to Nazism. Ask the people who lived through World War II if 'it can't happen here'.

How to prepare

Anyway, if you are going to prepare for an experience like this, it will depend if you are born in Australia or not born in Australia what is wrong with you.

IF YOU ARE NOT BORN IN AUSTRALIA

You'll be bugging out if you're heading here (Australia) because you currently aren't. You'll need to put the following things in your bug out bag.

1. Don't be born somewhere that is impacted by war or at any point falls under the control of a religious or military dictatorship. That is the first thing, put that in your bag. Be born in a prosperous Western democracy. Just do it.

2. If you must leave because your life is threatened for whatever reason, go back where you came from. You owe that to the people living wherever you tried to go apparently.

3. Be grateful for the taxpayer dollars that are being spent to deprive you of your liberty and of your chance for a decent life. That shitty TV in the rec room, the inedible sometimes salmonellesque food and the deliberately inadequate health care are gifts from the Australian people, and if you are not hugely grateful you should go back to where you came from again. And polls show the Australian people don't care what happens to you. Thanks for that Rupert Murdoch and all your evil little wizards.

IF YOU ARE BORN IN AUSTRALIA

You'll be bugging in. So how do you prepare for having your heart broken and your faith in your fellow citizens smashed? How do you prepare to resist the slow grind of powerlessness at the deliberate daily cruelty and lies and misinformation? Horror and despair at the bloodied money that changes hands. How do you prepare to watch your love for the country of your birth slowly wither? Put that in your bug out bag. Also, fresh towels, apparently they taste like chicken.

Eaten Fish

The true story of a rescue dog

The nice man from the dog rescue service brought her to our house. She was a funny looking little thing with filthy matted fur and an indescribably terrible smell.

> We took her straight from the puppy farm to the vet to be desexed so she has stitches. You can't give her a bath for a week.

> Sorry about the smell

thump thump

The stink was unbelievable. 8 Years in a cage in a puppy mill without a bath. He said her name was Gwyneth. It wasn't though, she had never had a name until the rescue service named her Gwyneth 2 days earlier.

wag wag

Our job was to foster Gwyneth until the rescue service could find her a home. They warned us that foster dogs are often frightened and broken. Locked in filthy cages their whole lives they didn't even know how to be dogs.

Not Gwyneth. Right away she was happy to meet us. Happy to get up on the furniture even though she smelled like satan's bottom. Excited to go for walks. Every meal was the best thing that had ever happened.

> This is breakfast? Every day?! OH MY GOD THIS IS FANTASTIC!

munch munch

SPINS AROUND WITH EXCITEMENT 3 TIMES BEFORE EATING

We counted the hours until she could have a bath. Aside from the stink she was very charming. Although not everyone was on board with the program.

> Aloha!

> You smell fascinating

> What fresh hell is this?!

FOOF!

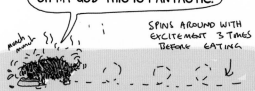

www.firstdogonthemoon.com

Puppy factory dogs live in overcrowded filthy conditions their whole lives, all they do is have puppies. It is all legal. When they're no longer productive they're shot or hit over the head. They know only cruelty and neglect

Unless they go to a rescue dog service!

After Gwyneth had her stitches out she had a very long soapy bath and a visit with the blow dryer. Suddenly a giant fluffball was sprinting around our house with excitement. Half an hour later she passed out in the cat's bed.

Z Z Z Z Z Z Z Z

We are keeping her even though she snores. We will call her Beyonce.

---

www.oscarslaw.org #adoptdontshop

CHAPTER 8

Death of a loved one

What is it?

My dog died. All these other apocali haven't happened or are happening to other people. But my dog died and this is my own small personal apocalypse. The weight of it changed me for ever. I am crushed and branded, down into nowhere and think I might never return.

What will happen? (death)

Death happens what can you do, once it has turned up to ruin everything not really much. Funerals are for the living etc etc. However during an apocalypse how we respond can make the difference between more other death turning up or hopefully avoiding it for a bit longer. Is it a zombie apocalypse that has just killed your companion? You should probably run away some more. Is it an asteroid that has thrown the Earth into an ice age? If the Earth isn't frozen and you cared about the person who just shuffled off their mortal etc you can probably take a moment to bury them. Maybe. I don't know, results may vary. Is it a Cormac McCartneyocalypse and everyone is a cannibal now? Well... that is something to think about isn't it?

The vet called to tell us that the weird swelling above the old dog's eye is an inoperable tumour – she gives him three to six months.

Sure he is 15 years old and he has already lived longer than we thought he would. But that doesn't mean anything.

When the reality of death comes and the floor disappears the world is changed forever, suddenly sliced in two, there is the world before and the world after. Eventually forgetting what the before felt like and that moment of sadness one day realising that after has become normal, day to day this is what it is now. The forgetting really begins. Like when my dog died. It wasn't a world-ending apocalypse – except for the people who loved him because it certainly was.

When we got him Peanut was very tiny and very stupid. His mum was a whippet and dad was a long-legged Jack Russell. So he was tenuous and a bit dainty as whippets sometimes are, but also headstrong and fierce when required. Opinionated. Reserved.

When he was a year old he was cut open by the teeth of a kelpie in the dog park. Actual guts spilling out of him and the kelpie's owner slinking away, I caught them at the traffic lights waiting to cross the road. Eventually they agreed to pay half the vet bill. Only half! People are terrible.

He was old, so old at the end, we'd had a difficult night – the tumour that was slowly strangling him from inside his face had almost done its job. We weren't quite sure, but it was very sad, even though he was very slow and slept a great deal he was still there.

He had some blood around his nose most of the time, every now and then it would be a trickle, then a puddle and then nothing. Then one night he struggled to breathe, it was clear that the tumour had made it into his throat or lungs – we took him to the vet and they gave us strong drugs to help him sleep. We were exhausted and felt broken. I slept next to him on the couch – his ragged terrible breathing would wake us both through the night. My last night with my dear old friend. In the morning we decided – the vets would come in the afternoon. We took him to the dog park, and we lay on the grass in the shade, amongst the daisies and warm breezes. It was a beautiful day and I hated it. We took the ball but we weren't going to throw it for him, just to have it there. Beyonce was there, and we all just took the time to be together and say goodbye.

The vets came, I think we offered to make them tea. Peanut lay on the couch and we sat around him tears streaming down our faces. They shaved his arm, or leg, I don't know – whatever that one at the front is called. We fed him schmackos and gorgonzola while they inserted the catheter. During his illness he had taken much of his medicine shoved into a chunk of gorgonzola. He loved it ridiculously. Beyonce thought it was okay but if he is getting some I have to get some too. Then suddenly and more quickly than I wanted the stuff came sweeping up the tube and into his beautiful old veins, it really is a terrible bright green. He was so very very tired and after what had been a wonderful life I was so grateful he could have a dignified death surrounded by everyone who loved him. He simply closed his eyes and we wept and waited. Patting his lovely old fur which was soaked with our tears. He would have drowned if it hadn't been for the green death magic.

And then he was gone.

We stayed with him. Beyonce came and sniffed him. I think about dogs' noses a lot, I wonder how death smells to a rescue dog. We thanked our friends the vets and wept and wept. They picked him up in his old bed and took him out to their car, climbed in as we said goodbye and hugged them and hugged each other and then they drove away. And he was really gone.

A few weeks later we received a box containing his ashes. I think we put them next to the ashes of Billy the cat, his story is another tiny terrible apocalypse. We talked about how we would dispose of them, set them free (set ourselves free). Marieke had some of the ashes from her beautiful dog Bob Ellis put into ink and they became part of a tattoo. She is a magical creature though, I'm not sure I am a dog ash tattoo ink kind of person.

Peanut was not a demonstrative animal, he was always happy to see you with doggy enthusiasm but never hysterical. The older he got the less he bothered, but he had a refined and thoughtful manner. In his later years he didn't give a fuck about anything, it was fantastic considering his upbringing.

In his early years, he wasn't allowed to tear up pieces of paper – letters and things would end up on the floor, he would carefully extract tissues from the garbage and then shred them happily and surgically and then leave them for us to find. If he had done it while we were out, he would greet us at the door with that guilty dog wiggling and wagging. Later when his circumstances changed, it was pointed out that a) who cared if he tore up bits of paper? And b) look at how happy it makes him. And so he did. It became a game, he was given old bits of paper at every opportunity and tore them gaily into tiny pieces.

And every time I got down on my knees to pick some newspaper or kitchen towel out of the rug, I was grateful and happy. Sure cleaning up is a pain, but the dog was doing something he loved. It became a dog-based prayer later on, gratitude for being given permission to just enjoy things that were enjoyable.

After he died it wasn't the same for a long time. It still isn't. It's not just the drinking too much alcohol and getting fat. The joy went out of the cartoons. I would sit in front of the tablet, and where once some sparkling idiocy would bubble up into my brain, nothing would come. I would have to drag out dusty, tired ideas like bedsprings trapped under a pile of bricks and beat them into submission. It was grim for a long time. Things are better now but they will never be the same again.

What is the likelihood?

One hundred per cent your pets will die and so will you.

How to prepare

Live your best life and try not to be a dickhead.

What you will need

A dog.
To love the dog.
The dog to die.
Your heart will break
but you will be okay.

HOW I SURVIVED LIVING WITH A CAT STUFFED WITH URANIUM AND HOW THE CAT SURVIVED LIVING WITH ME.

Chu Chu had an overactive thyroid. Or maybe it was underactive. It was either hyperthyroidism or hypothyroidism the vet knew the difference between them and which one it was and told me. It made her INCREDIBLY fussy (Chu Chu not the vet) we would feed her six different things in a day, she would glare reproachfully and eat nothing she was getting thinner and thinner as we watched. We took her to the vet who said (after extensive EXPENSIVE blood tests, some phrenology and a thorough leeching), your cat [Chu Chu is a cat] has an over/underactive thyroid because of the hyper/hypothyroidism I am telling you this but you will not remember which is ok I am a vet and I have written it down. We were advised that there were two choices for Chu Chu, either tablets twice a day for the rest of her life or a radiation treatment which she would only need once but which would be expensive.

Three choices: the third we do nothing and she would slowly waste away. Not really an option even though she also had chronic cat flu which meant she sneezed a lot often on the back of your head and I know people don't think about cat snot a lot but in our house it is a common occurrence just thought I would share that. Cat snot is an evil substance not as bad as cat poop but more on that later. We calculated that if Chu Chu lived another five years, giving her enormous tablets twice a day would end up costing the same as the expensive radiation treatment and we would also have to give her enormous tablets twice a day. She was never going to die, but we might from being savaged by Chu Chu every time we tried to shove a pill down her gob while she covered our soon to be corpses in kitty nosemucus.

We sent her to the cat-radiating facility where she was to stay for a week. They said when she comes back from being radiated – that is what they do they blast the cat with radiation or bung a stick of plutonium up her Barnaby Joyce[18] or something idk – it is COMPLETELY safe they said, but just in case don't let her sit on any pregnant people and avoid her poop and also HER SNOT IS RADIOACTIVE. (They didn't say the last bit but we already knew that).

The interesting thing about radioactive cat poop (I bet you didn't think you would read that sentence today) is that our rescue dog Beyonce loves to eat cat poop more than anything else and doesn't it sound like a fun time at our house? As I mentioned Roy the rescue border collie is on Prozac but that is for another time. Cat-poop eating is Beyonce's only character flaw she spent eight years in a cage at a puppy mill what are you going to do. She follows the cat around like it is a food truck or a Mr Whippy. We said to the vet, can you please keep Chu Chu in the lead-lined cat bunker for an extra week we will pay because we are very fond of Beyonce and we don't want her to get some sort of weird cat excreta-related cancer. And they did. Chu Chu came home and she was fine except she is still very fussy and still covers everything with cat snoutgloop or whatever it is that comes out of the front of her face. Beyonce was very happy to see her. Interestingly Chu Chu is on steroids now for her chronic cat flu and we have to give her the tablets twice a day for the rest of her life. The end.

CHAPTER 9

Nuclear war

What is it?

NUCLEAR WAR OMG! ACTUAL NUCLEAR WAR IN WHICH MORE THAN ONE NATION FIRES A BUNCH OF NUCLEAR MISSILES AT EACH OTHER. There are approximately 17,000 nuclear weapons in the world at the moment. Hi guys stay where you are please.

What will happen?

It all depends on the size of the conflagration and the location. Dropping one (1) smallish 'nuke' would be really bad for the people under it and near it but it is possible that might sort of be all that happens because everyone else would freak out so thoroughly. It is not one of those cut-and-dried situations where everybody who doesn't die straight away dies eventually on Earth anyway. Or do they?

Let's say one of the nations that currently has nuclear weapons – Russia, the United States, China, India, Israel, France, North Korea, Queanbeyan, Pakistan and the United Kingdom – fires some of their nuclear weapons at one or other of those aforementioned nations or even near one of them or in such a way that one of these other nations thinks 'those bastards' and fires a few back and then woooo it is on like Donkey Kong was a terrible person who had never heard of Dian Fossey.

Depending on the targets and the size of the war hundreds of thousands to millions will probably die immediately. There will be massive MASSIVE firestorms that will burn tens or hundreds of thousands or millions of square kilometres and send huge clouds of poisonous black carbon into

Well actually, the "science" of "global warming" isn't "settled"

Ian the Climate Denialist Potato

the stratosphere where it will block out most of the sun possibly for years. A big conflagration will postpone global warming for a while so that's nice! Thanks clouds!

However in a nuclear winter there's a lot less rain but also much more famine and disease everywhere. That sort of thing. There would be approximately a metric fucktonne of radioactive fallout that would spread globally along with enormous clouds (boooo clouds) of toxic chemical death smoke that would float about the place. Gross. It will either be terrible, really terrible or so terrible it ruins everything (EVERYTHING).

What is the likelihood?

I have no fucking idea any more. I remember when the Cold War was over and it seemed most of the bombier countries like the United States and Russia and China didn't get rid of all of their nukes but at least they stopped banging on about it. Pakistan and India are certainly a worry. Iran seems to have slowed it down a bit but now with Trump carrying on who knows although by the time this book is published he might have been replaced by the Milkshake Duck... oh wait.[19] The list of people Trump hasn't antagonised is shorter than the list of those he has. And North Korea did I mention North Korea? So the idea of Mutually Assured Destruction which is supposed to be a sufficient deterrent I suspect it probably is unless the person with their finger hovering above the button is a sociopath with the humanity of a banana. The Prognostotron has rated it a maybe because it doesn't know either.

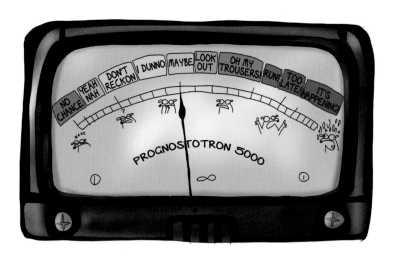

How to prepare

I read a *Guardian* article (of course I did) that said the best place to be in case there is a nuclear war is Antarctica! But you will have to dress and live as a penguin if you want to find community. Or you could go to Easter Island in the South Pacific. Or Kiribati or the Marshall Islands which really are a long way away from a lot of places except the poisoned sea and the death-filled sky.

This is one apocalyptic scenario that really needs a serious bunker – depending on where you are, you will need to stay away from radioactivity for hmmmm let's see a gazillion years or some such.

Radioactive fallout can be a problem for years – but unless you are in a directly impacted area you might come out after two to four weeks but then you might be dead anyway, or not, I read a lot about this it is awful. Too horrible to put it all here. If it is a really bad nuclear war, a properly sealed shelter with many years of food and water and supplies probably won't even be enough. If it is a smallish conflagration in a different hemisphere to yours, there would still be a bit of the old nuclear winter action and radioactive fallout hoofing about the globe so you know…[20] The global economy still collapses as does the capacity for the Earth to produce enough food for white people. That bunker will need to be real solid.

Also there is a difference in various types of nuclear explosions 'dirty' 'clean' etc. and the worst of all seems to be what happens with a nuclear power plant – that stuff will fukushima you up ahahahaha nuclear meltdown joke. Sorry. Where you are in relation to it all is critical. Also get some iodine in case your cat gets an overactive thyroid. Or is it an underactive thyroid? I can't remember. It is an underachieving cat whatever the diagnosis.

CHAPTER 10

Asteroids!

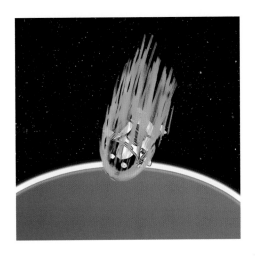

What is it!

ASTEROIDS! WOOOO SO EXCITING FROM SPACE!

You can finally relax a bit this one is really really unlikely – even if an asteroid big enough to destroy civilisation is planning to crash into the Earth we might (might) have enough time to build a rocket and crash Bruce Willis into it. (The asteroid not the rocket.)

NASA reckons we should build that rocket now just in case but they would say that. Science tells us that if the asteroid that crashed into the Earth 66 million years ago killing the dinosaurs had been thirty seconds earlier or later it would have missed and you could have a triceratops in your greenhouse right now (not a euphemism) or even as prime minister.

That is because the Earth is moving through space at 107,000 kilometres per hour which makes it an extremely moving target for a weeny 10-kilometre-wide asteroid. If that asteroid hadn't been destroyed in the cataclysm I would have told it to go out and buy a bunch of lottery tickets because the chances of it whacking into the Earth were v slim which is good news because that is the one thing which could in fact completely destroy life on Earth without any effort at all. It depends on the size – if it was really really big then it might even destroy the whole actual planet! That would be extremely exciting albeit with a sad ending. I would watch that movie. If it was a 'smaller' one like the one that killed the dinosaurs when it hurtled spacely into what would become Mexico a bunch of terrible things would happen. They called that the Chicxulub asteroid, it arrived at the end of the Cretaceous and ruined a lot of people's (large lizard's) day.

What will happen?

Firstly there will be a huge shockwave that destroys everything it waves at blasting debris into the sky all of which would rain back down on the Earth in a big rain of hot firey wreckage that would get filth all over your washing. You would have to do it again except there would be a firestorm all around the Earth which would kill pretty much everything that wasn't underground. Is your laundry underground? No it is not. You'll never need change for the laundromat ever again because your underpants are on fire and so is the rest of you. And who really wants to survive that tbh and that is probably what the dinosaurs thought too as their underpants burst into flames.

Then there would be an ice age because of all the dust in the sky similar to a nuclear war but far less anthropogenic.

What is the likelihood? (not very)

Asteroids with a one-kilometre (0.62 mi) diameter strike Earth every 500,000 years on average so you know…

How to prepare

First watch *Armageddon* and *Deep Impact* – watching these movies won't really help at all but *Deep Impact* has a tidal wave in it who doesn't love a tidal wave movie? I know I do. Also,[21] Bruce Willis and Ben Affleck die when they crash a rocket into an asteroid in *Armageddon* to save the Earth so there is no downside there either.

Also *The Day After Tomorrow* is good but that is a movie about bad weather which ends the world not entirely relevant to this scenario but climate scientists think it is not entirely impossible and it has a great tidal wave too. I think they should make more movies about the weather – have you seen *Perfect Storm*? OMG George Clooney in a boat.

For a middle-sized asteroid impact you probably need to be a) underground (firestorm and rain of hot debris) and b) way above sea level (tsunami and/or tidal wave). And if there is a mini-ice age you might need to be near the equator or not. Society will probably collapse you will need a lot of food water and an enormous can of asteroid repellent. Asteroff or even Armageddaway! Ahahaahah note to editor please make sure these jokes do not end up in the book.

HOW I SURVIVED BY NOT BEING A LESSER STICK-NEST RAT

I love the greater stick-nest rat (*Leporillus conditor*). It builds a big stick nest with its friends and they live in it. It is an enormous (almost thirty-centimetre-long) fat rat that sits on its hind legs like a bunny. The lesser stick-nest rat (*Leporillus apicalis*), which I also love, is extinct. They weren't as big as the greater stick-nest rat, but they would also build large communal nests. They are gone now. So many are gone now.

GREATER STICK NEST RAT

CHAPTER 11

Extinction Level Event

What is it? This is every animal that has become extinct in Australia since European settlement. It is a cautionary tail of what happens when one fails to plan for the unexpected (if you are a bird, mammal, lizard, frog or snalug). This list is based on information from the internet so it is quite possibly wrong. Confirming extinction, (like using the internet) is an inexact science, but unfortunately this is probably still mostly sort of accurate.

What will happen? It will keep happening.

Likelihood – 100% and still happening.

How to prepare? No time to prepare it is happening to creatures everywhere right now while you are reading this.

18
(Artists impression - no image available)

1 Tasman starling (Aplonis fusca) 2 Lord Howe pigeon (Columba vitiensis godmanae) 3 Lord Howe parakeet (Cyanoramphus subflavescens) 4 Western rufous bristlebird (Dasyornis broadbenti litoralis) 5 King Island emu (Dromaius novaehollandiae minor) 6 Kangaroo Island emu (Dromaius baudinianus) 7 Tasmanian emu (Dromaius novaehollandiae diemenensis) 8 Norfolk ground dove (Alopecoenas norfolkensis) 9 Lord Howe gerygone (Gerygone insularis) 10 Norfolk Island pigeon (Hemiphaga novaeseelandiae spadicea) 11 Norfolk triller (Lalage leucopyga leucopyga) 12 Norfolk kaka (Nestor productus) 13 Lord Howe boobook (Ninox novaeseelandiae albaria) 14 Norfolk boobook (Ninox novaeseelandiae undulata) 15 Lord Howe swamphen (Porphyrio albus) 16 Paradise parrot (Psephotellus pulcherrimus) 17 Western Lewin's rail (Lewinia pectoralis clelandi) 18 Macquarie Island rail (Gallirallus philippensis macquariensis) 19 Lord Howe fantail (Rhipidura fuliginosa cervina) 20 Norfolk thrush (Turdus poliocephalus poliocephalus) 21 Lord How Island Thrush (Turdus poliocephalus vinitinctus) 22 White-chested white-eye (Zosterops albogularis) 23 Robust white-eye (Zosterops strenuus) 24 Southern gastric-brooding frog (Rheobatrachus silus) 25 Northern gastric-brooding frog (Rheobatrachus vitellinus) 26 Mount Glorious day frog (Taudactylus diurnus)

27 Campbell's Land Snail (Advena campbelli) 28 Norfolk Snail (Nancibella quintalia)
29 Lord Howe Snail (Tornelasmias capricorni) 30 Macquarie Slug (Angrobia
dulvertonensis) 31 Lord Howe Slug (Placostylus bivaricosus etheridgei)
32 Lake Pedder Earthworm (Hypolimnus pedderensis) 33 Desert rat-kangaroo
(Caloprymnus campestris) 34 Pig-footed bandicoot (Chaeropus ecaudatus) 35
White-footed rabbit-rat (Conilurus albipes) 36 Lake Mackay hare-wallaby
(Lagorchestes asomatus) 37 Rufous hare-wallaby (Lagorchestes hirsutus)
38 Eastern hare-wallaby (Lagorchestes leporides) 39 Toolache wallaby
(Macropus greyi) 40 Lesser bilby (Macrotis leucura) 41 Bramble Cay melomys
(Melomys rubicola) 42 Long-tailed hopping mouse (Notomys longicaudatus
43 Big-eared hopping mouse (Notomys macrotis) 44 Darling Downs hopping mouse
(Notomys mordax) 45 Crescent nail-tail wallaby (Onychogalea lunata)
46 Desert bandicoot (Perameles eremiana) 47 Broad-faced potoroo (Potorous platyops)
48 Blue-grey mouse (Pseudomys glaucus) 49 Gould's mouse (Pseudomys gouldii)
50 Dusky flying fox (Pteropus brunneus) 51 Maclear's rat (Rattus macleari)
52 Bulldog rat (Rattus nativitatis) 53 Thylacine (Thylacinus cynocephalus)
54 Lesser stick-nest rat (Leporillus apicalis)

HOW I SURVIVED BEING A NOT VERY GOOD FREELANCE CARTOONIST

I always wanted to be an actor but went into cartooning because you can do it by yourself and you only need paper and a pen. Acting involves all sorts of other things, especially people who are always making things more complicated than they need to be.

After my mum died in 1995 I went a bit mad – that is normal apparently. I didn't draw anything for five years and was drifting slowly toward giving up even trying to be a cartoonist. Who wants to be an aspiring cartoonist when you're middle aged and a bit broken and squished by life? Then I ended up in Melbourne where I fell in love with AFL footy. My boss at the time said, 'Get an AFL team, it doesn't matter who'. So I did. (The Western Bulldogs). I have a lot of opinions and feelings about this particular sport but more on that another time.[22]

I gave cartooning one last shot – I bought a tiny Wacom drawing tablet and started doing a few cartoons about the Western Bulldogs AFL team. I posted them on bigfooty.com where they got noticed and enjoyed and it gave me the motivation to continue. Eventually, I sent them to a man named Jonathan Green the editor of a disreputable news website. He ignored them. I sent them again because I knew how to be a freelancer, and he sent me an email saying 'you are a funny man'. The rest is not particularly interesting history but history it is.

This was October 2007, the Australian Federal election was on, bringing with it (we hoped) the end of ten years of a grim conservatism that didn't entirely smash the country to bits, (although, if you ask the people on the receiving end of the NT intervention they may have a different view). But John Howard and his crew of scaly mates certainly went a long way to grinding the country down into various pieces. It was a government of pompous born-to-rule shysters, dead-hearted dog-whistlers and bloodless sneaks who took great pleasure in turning anything they could get their claws on into a rusty political shiv to stick in their ideological enemies (mainly poor people, women, anyone in the LGBTQI community, Aboriginal Australians).

Twas ever thus. It made me extremely cross and I drew many hilarious/furious cartoons about it all. I even won a Walkley. So it worked out for me I'll be right jack.

Did I mention I won a Walkley?

CHAPTER 12

FOOD or not

(see also Bees!)

What is it?

Imagine a world where you could no longer have pineapple on your pizza!

Imagine a world where the only thing in the supermarket is the unmurderable eggplant, widely accepted by decent folk everywhere as the cockroach of the vegetable universe. Imagine if every meal consisted of the purple squishy terror – cough *dystopian hellscape* cough. Is it a plant? Is it an egg? Neither, it is an atrocity masquerading as food and is undeniable proof there is no God.

Other than the clear existential threat of eggplant, how good is Food?! Sure, there are food shortages all over the globe right now a child dies of starvation every ten seconds. But we're not talking about THOSE food shortages. And we are not talking about the United States where five per cent of all households struggle to provide enough food for the people sitting around the table like some not properly thought through Norman Rockwell painting. We have enough to feed everyone on Earth right now but you know we are busy and important we have things to do. This particular apocalypse is the kind of global food shortage that inconveniences everyone (you dear reader, et moi) by collapsing the economy of this or that country or somehow making actual numerous different kinds of food unavailable and increasing prices for EVERYONE! (e.g. you and me again unless you like eggplant in which case you get everything you deserve).

Climate change is the main culprit EXCEPT IT ISN'T REAL! Just kidding of course it is.

no it isn't

A warming planet leads to less food. Did you know that climate change affects how farmers plan for the upcoming year? Of course it does now that you think

about it. According to a fancy report that I did not read from the completely discredited Intergovernmental Panel on Climate Change, every decade of global warming reduces the amount of food the world can produce by two per cent. Not an immediate threat, so relax.

But there are other things

What about DROUGHTS! Obviously, you can't grow eggplants in a drought and why would you? When droughts start affecting the less droughtier places the less growinger they are, unless you mean FLOODS which are okay if you grow underwater eggplants (this is a real thing they are carnivorous and prefer the flesh of tiny children). A flood OR drought will ruin your day as a plant-growing person (farmer), whereas a simultaneous flood AND drought will erm… thinking face.

Then there is EXTREME WEATHER! Cyclones, blizzards, children's birthday parties all these things make it harder to grow crops and keep your elk inside the compound.

COLLAPSING FISHERIES! We take too many fish from the sea and various fish communities have collapsed at various times as well. Did you know there are underwater heatwaves? True! Warming oceans killed the Great Barrier Reef and also huge kelp forests and the sorts of things that keep fish alive. Coral reefs support around a quarter of all marine life. We are so fucked it is not even funny.

The amount of fish (trillions) that we catch in a year would reach to the sun and back if you put them all end to end.

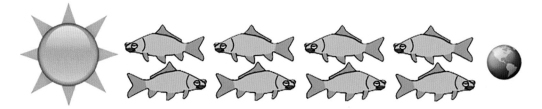

Unlike many of the other 'true' things in this book this fact is actually true – look it up. Plankton are the foundation for the entire ocean food chain and have been declining steadily for years possibly (probably) because of global warming. If they all die we will

A plankton → ·

Another plankton → ·

Their friend → ·

have dead seas, no fish and a rapid build up of C02 in the atmosphere. MORE CARBON! As one scientist said[23] These tiny creatures do the 'lion's share' of sustaining life on Earth and they're dying out. Ocean acidification is ruining everything as well. There is a thousand mile stretch of ocean just off Namibia where hydrogen sulphide is just bubbling out of the ocean as a result of all this kerfuffle. Stand by, more coming. Just fyi.

What will happen?

You won't be able to have pineapple on your pizza. Or prawns. There may be food riots. I know I would kick the living shit out of the bin outside my local pizza place if they were like 'pineapple is extinct sorry'. Cities will be bad places to be but then so will the country. Martial law might be declared, it depends on the nature of the shortage (no more pineapple/plague of eggplant). If there is a famine people go to where they think there might be food and if there isn't any there they starve to death.

This is a hard apocalypse to make fun of really because it is the reality for so many people on Earth right now as you read this. It would be a lot more fun if it was an asteroid or alien eggplant invasion.

What is the likelihood?

Will any of these things happen this week? Probably not, but they will happen, and if enough of them happen at the same time the SCHTFBT! You heard me TSCHTFBT! TS![24]

How to prepare

You will need to a) have plenty of sustenance already safely stored, and b) somewhere to grow your own food, which c) you are able to protect from all the people who can't do a and b. You need a secret hideout like Captain Midnite the bushranger had in the book by Randolph Stow. I loved that book.

CHAPTER 13

The apocalypse of Political Correctness

(Culturally Marxist)

Welcome to the Bitter Frightened Angry Old White Man Show with your host

Andreas Poffertje

I'm angry!

What is it?

The pervasive creep of political correctness is the thin end of the slippery slope down which free speech slithers as it withers! Wheeee! Political correctness is global warming to the arctic ice shelf of freedom. Making its way lurkingly through the fabric of our governments, institutions, schools and media, this sinister agenda infiltrates our everyday normal white-people lives as older men and our families also women. It is an underhanded totalitarian program being implemented by cunning ELITES (cultural Marxists and their bearded literati pals) which consists primarily of telling people to shut the fuck up when they say racist or sexist or homophobic things it is the very unravelling of civilisation as we have gotten used to it. Christmas? BANNED. Easter? BANNED. SHARIA LAW? Tolerated if not openly encouraged I don't even know what it is but I don't like it. Everything is all identity politics and intersectionalism and reverse racism against white male media commentators and politicians who these days are one of the most marginalised groups since Jesus was a girl.

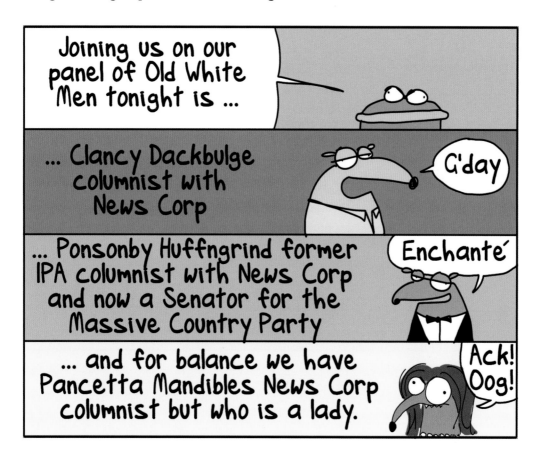

There is a war on normality with unisex toilets and you're not allowed to wear black face anymore which is a national past time here in Australia it is mentioned in our national anthem. Meanwhile in the United States you can't even have a Klan rally outside a mosque any more what is the world coming to? (Actually, you probably can now.)

What will happen?

White genocide is coming! Finally! What a relief. Well, at least some good will come of this, and isn't that something to look forward to? White people are terrible all these plonkers who are complaining about free speech really

want to do is say the n word on national television and now they are living in a gulag instead. Sad. Let's face it, totalitarianism is bad but that's not what political correctness really is. When someone complains about political correctness they're not describing something. It is, as they say, a verbal Swiss army knife for making things you disagree with go away. Once it has been called political correctness or fake news or Jeb Bush, it can be dismissed as trivial and frivolous. Please clap. It will get to a point where if you call women 'fat pigs,' 'dogs,' 'slobs,' and 'disgusting animals' and talk about 'grabbing pussy', if you call Mexicans rapists and drug dealers, you will no longer be able to become President of the United States. That is the sort of freedom being whisked away from us (WHISKED) by the clammy claws of elitist do-gooderés and the Aboriginal Industry with their freedom whisks. If you can't draw obviously racist caricatures of Aboriginal people and bravely take credit for starting a national conversation about the behaviour of Aboriginal people because it is in their best interest, you are being oppressed by political correctness and the left. Complaining about white people being racist is also racist. Let's fly the Earth into the Sun now.

What is the likelihood?

It is already here. Cultural Marxism (which is code for JEWS DID THIS) has been around since World War II when it was made up in the 1980s. Marxist Jewish academics fled to the United States after the war to undermine it with their Marxist notions those ungrateful bastards. How do you know if you are impacted by Cultural Marxism? You don't until it is TOO LATE! Although, if you have ever read any liberal media, gone to school or read any of the internet, it is possible you have been affected and infected. Come to think of it you are reading some THIS VERY SECOND AHAHAHAH you are a communist now congratulations comrade!

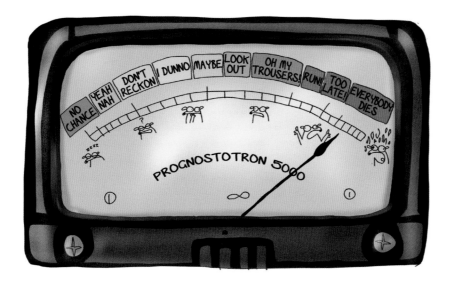

How to prepare

Get in your bunker now and stay there because the rainbow Reich feminazis are coming your way. It's even better if you have a crawlspace, line it with screen grabs you printed out from the MRA pepe kek youtube supercuts channel. Other than that do not read anything ever. If you do have to read more make sure it is a Murdoch owned media publication (like this one I am not even joking, who knew ABC books was licensed to those bastards

at HarperCollins – jfc I am such a hypocrite). Free speech is touted by News Corp commenters as the holy grail of western civilisation even though when they're not fluffing for Rupert these culture war Horst Wessels spend their weekends crying into their Campari and soda working out how much they will make for suing people who mildly slagged them off under Australia's ludicrous (and genuinely) free speech inhibiting libel laws. Is there anyone more litigious than a News Corp columnist? If there is we don't know because they always insist on a confidentiality clause. I'm enjoying how ranty and weird this book is getting now and so should you.

HOW I SURVIVED BEING THE CHILD OF A WHITE WOMAN WHO DOCUMENTED RACISM WITH HER PAINTING

As told to F Onthemoon by F Onthemoon's Dad, Grandpa Onthemoon.

My pre-me family moved to Bega from Townsville in 1963 and stayed there until 1969. Dad (John) worked in the local hospital while Mum (Patricia, always known as Paddy) was a very #busymum with my brothers-to-be Jeremy and Simon already going to school when she gave birth to me, Tiny Onthemoon, on Good Friday, April 1965. (They called me 'Little Easter' because they couldn't agree on what to call me. Nicholas was one possibility. If I had been a girl I would have been Penelope and I think Mum was disappointed I wasn't a girl and haven't I spent a lot of time in therapy talking about that let me tell you, anyway I digress).

Life in Bega in the 60s was very hectic, everyone was involved in various things like the recently opened Bega Preschool,[25] the Tathra Surf Life Saving Club, the local branch of the Australian Labor Party and the Bega Valley Fine Art Society which inspired Paddy to get back in to painting. Mum graduated in 1956 as a secondary school art teacher in Victoria, and had earlier been a foundation member of the Townsville Art Society as well as going on telly in Townsville with a show called *Painting with Paddy* (or maybe Patti). If anyone has tapes of that (nobody does) I will give you actual money.

Mum did some teaching at Bega High School as well. The Bega Valley Fine Art Society was a very conservative group, so when she exhibited six paintings in the Society's annual exhibition in 1965, there were, as Dad said, 'rumblings that her work was perhaps, not appropriate.'

Paddy's paintings of the local Aboriginal people showed how impoverished and dreadful their living conditions were. Bega in those days was very much a 'cow town' – everything revolved around dairy farming. The Bega River ran through the valley with rich river flats along each side. These river flats were home to lush grass paddocks for dairy cattle, but also great for bean growing, and this was the exploitative connection with the local Aboriginal people, who were employed to pick the beans by hand – hard, back-breaking work. They often lived near or on some of the properties in conditions that were at best third world, as one of Mum's pen and wash drawings shows for example, living in old car bodies.

Mum's paintings had titles such as 'Seasonal Workers' Huts', 'Fringe Dwellers', 'Children Playing'. Dad tells the story of how one very active member of the Bega Valley Fine Art Society, and also the wife of one of the district's leading bean farmers, said in a very loud voice when she arrived at the 1965 exhibition 'Why on earth is Paddy painting these people?'

Dad reckons Paddy wasn't prepared to hide her concern for the plight of the local Aboriginal people and was unafraid to make a political comment in a very conservative country town in 1965. It sounds like a not very good movie starring Jackie Weaver and Bill Hunter, but there you are, this was my Mum. Mum was a legend and how good are white people! So good.

Me, Paddy and Paddy's granddaughter Ruby.

CHAPTER 14

Invasion!

ALWAYS WAS, ALWAYS WILL BE ABORIGINAL LAND

What is it?

If you really want to talk about apocalypse.

This is hard to write, I assume it is going to sound racist and weird. I am pretty sure it is automatically racist anyway because I am writing it on stolen land. I'm white and I grew up in Australia. I learned, like all settler Australians do, to live with the treatment of Aboriginal people in this country. That doesn't mean I ever agreed with it, it doesn't mean I didn't rail against it, it was always wrong, always a great injustice, and all the while seemingly intractable. But it also just was. This is the racism at the heart of Australia, the sad ease with which the brutal invasion of this country by Europeans is accepted, even gleefully denied. It is also typical of how the history of Aboriginal Australia is viewed: on this land for more than 80,000 years, the oldest living culture in the world, a bloody war of dispossession in which hundreds of thousands died and here I am talking about my white person feelings. To be fair to me, I am at least consistent in that all I ever do is talk about my white-person feelings (as a #notallmen man). In fact, I make quite a good living out of it thank you. But in this instance, I'm not alone in putting myself, my whiteness, at the centre of the understanding of the history and the current circumstance of Indigenous Australians. And this really was (is) an apocalypse.

It was long thought that more than 20,000 people died in our Frontier Wars. Recent research suggests well over 65,000 Aboriginal people may have been killed in Queensland alone.

That is more Australians than died in WW1

What will happen?

Fifty thousand years ago – more than 80,000 years – imagine dear reader (if you aren't an Aboriginal Australian) if your family, your community, had lived in the same region of a particular country for 80,000 years. Imagine that you had clear abiding links to the land and the people and the stories, that you had been working and managing and living on that land for 80,000 years. Fifty thousand years. I have trouble remembering the 80s, but I still feel a fondness for my childhood home. I googled it just now and the bastards have knocked it down to build some townhouses and I can tell you I was a bit upset.

We only lived there for fifteen years or so, then the family sort of split up and we all went our various ways. We sold it and got money for it, but it was still our home for fifteen years and I had feelings when I saw it gone.

How does it feel if you and your family, everyone you ever knew for more generations than I can even comprehend (3500?) have lived on the same country for 80,000 years and then one day people come along and try to move you off it. And when you refuse, they kill your family, they corral you like the beasts they think you are and your people die in their thousands, in a brutal bloody war of dispossession. And they just take all of your land.

What is the likelihood?

One hundred per cent.

How to prepare

How would I feel if that had been my family's home for 50,000 years and they came and built ugly townhouses on it and shot my dad? I reckon we should cut Aboriginal people some slack, which is very gracious of me I know. Not only has all this terrible stuff been done to them for over 200 years, the descendants of the people who started it the people who are still doing it sit around telling them it didn't really happen like that and even if it did which it didn't they should get over it be grateful and assimilate. Fuck colonialism seriously.

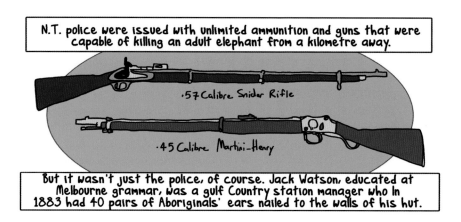

N.T. police were issued with unlimited ammunition and guns that were capable of killing an adult elephant from a kilometre away.

.57 Calibre Snider Rifle

.45 Calibre Martini-Henry

But it wasn't just the police, of course. Jack Watson, educated at Melbourne grammar, was a gulf Country station manager who In 1883 had 40 pairs of Aboriginals' ears nailed to the walls of his hut.

How rude (racist) is it for white people to be worried about the apocalypse when they have already inflicted one on a group of people and refuse to acknowledge it? We are freaking out about how much we have to lose when we stole it anyway! You can tell I have a lot of feelings about it, about us white people shambling about like puffy blind pallid ghosts on the land our forebears stole, sure we didn't do it with our own hands but we live on it every day.

I don't know what we need to do (a treaty and paying the rent would be a start, asking Aboriginal people what they reckon and ACTUALLY LISTENING TO THE ANSWER would be a start) it is never going to be a question that white people can answer. We are in possession of stolen goods. Australia as they say is a crime scene.*

We like to erase Aboriginal people, talk about what their culture *was* like what they *were* like even though Indigenous Australians are living here now. Today. Aboriginal people want their land back it was never ceded, and we take the easy way out, spending our time debating 'Are we a racist nation? What is racism anyway?' rather than actually doing something, anything about the racism.

We still don't call it a war. It was a 150 year long series of skirmishes that left possibly more than 100,000 people dead.

---

* They being an Aboriginal bloke speaking at a demonstration I was at and it was such a good line I stole it. No shame.

HOW I SURVIVED BEING A SELF-PROCLAIMED NATIONAL TREASURE

I thoroughly enjoyed the spectacle of a political thresher shark like John Howard losing his dogwhistle cunning (and his seat). Sure his progressive replacement Kevin Rudd was your least favourite uncle, but he wasn't John Howard. Or was he? No he wasn't. Alright he was a bit.

Democracy was only with us for a short time. Yet it sparkled the bright sparkle of freedom.

After being on the sidelines for so many years – I was finally a player! No longer a gormless observer like most of the populace (you dear reader), I was thrust into the midst of the maelstrom of democracy, rubbing shoulders with the political class[26] and media heavyweights. I was a full-time political cartoonist (albeit on a tiny, not very good news website[27]) and here was my chance to have an impact, to make myself the story, which is what all the really good cartoonists and journalists do these days. My particular take on the politics of the day involved marsupials and talking vegetables and not being able to draw people and it struck a chord with decent leftists across the nation.

I was well on my way to being a self-proclaimed national treasure and running my very own think tank, The First Dog on the Moon Institute. I met prime ministers, got invited to fancy parties. Right-wing columnists railed against me! I won awards and accolades and became one of the most loved and yet humble progressive figures in the country. An elite!

I joined the literati and the twitterati and 'finally' allowed myself to become firmly convinced of my own fabulousness. I had made it! All deserved of course, I was having a lovely time, OR WAS I?! Perhaps there was a hidden truth, that I was dead inside, a hollowed-out shell wracked with fear that I had betrayed everything I believed in, a fraudulent hypocrite.

Ahahahahaha, no I was fabulous and completely deserved everything. I still do and yet remain disarmingly humble. It is a gift.

Unbeknownst to me – a self-described well-meaning anarcho marsupialist – I would become a guiding light of the rising progressive class.[28] We were the remora sliding after the politicians and party hacks. We were content creators, commentators, startup nerds, lawyers who joined the Greens and failed vegans who could afford to buy houses (Gen X). We were able to spend our time concerned (legitimately so I might add) with all manner of injustices without really threatening the status quo. Oh, I've hated capitalism all my life – but it's been good to me. Seems a little ungracious really – anyway I was unwittingly reproducing existing economic and social relations because why the fuck wouldn't I?! What else are you going to do?

CHAPTER 15

Capitalism

What is it and what will happen?

The means of production (all the stuff) will be owned by a few people who will make an enormous amount of money, some other people will make bit of money (cartoonists, accountants, people who run chicken shops and so on) and many many more will go without. It will be a humongous self-replicating machine for the creation of self-justification and delicious snacks within an interlocking system of extraordinary smugness that will ultimately destroy the planet and the human race for the benefit of shareholders who didn't even do any of the work.

It will seem like a good idea at the time until it doesn't and by then it will be too late anyway. The wealth will be incredible! And the poverty will be literally unimaginable (unless you have experienced it, in which case it will sit in your gut your whole life). The role of government will be to stay out of the way and do all the things that you can't make money out of which isn't much these days and they will mostly bugger that up because the government will be run by people who are supposed to be taking a break from being capitalists but you can't ever really do that.

What is the likelihood?

It's happening!

How to prepare

Too late! Run. What you will need to survive or even thrive:

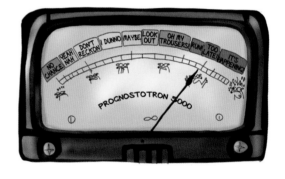

Either be born into wealth or acquire it through good fortune or criminal activity (sometimes it can be done with just the sweat of your brow and a can-do attitude, but who am I kidding that is what they will tell you it is not true).

Or prepare for a life of mostly thankless toil and to never imagine the life you might have had, the person you might have been if you didn't have to struggle every day to make a life for you and your family.

Although... what if you only struggled and sacrificed because you chose to, and you did it so you could do or be something completely awesome and unexpected? Imagine! No. Even if you have a job and do okay, your boss still gets to tell you what to do and you have no real say in it. There's no real democracy at work. Even if you are a capitalist you're not free because you have to be a capitalist, you have to make a profit.

If that doesn't work, how about bringing capitalism to an end by tricking people into using democracy to usher in a golden age of socialism! Polls show that we will be popular if we plan to nationalise the banks and eat the rich! (I have heard they taste like chicken.)

Alright we won't eat them we'll throw them in the sea (the shallow bit). By the time they're out, we will have collectivised all their stuff and they will have to live in a caravan.[29] And the radical centrists will be put in a rocket and sent to live on Pluto which isn't even a planet.

Sending the radical centrists to Pluto.

And don't come back!

Work with me here – once you accept that capitalism doesn't work then ipso facto you have to accept that something will need to replace it – unless it kills us all first, which it probably will. Many people will tell you that capitalism of one variety or another or some

ipso facto

finagling of the free market will be okay and a rising tide lifts all boats, but that isn't true and don't listen to anyone who says it is they are wrong.[30] Because we can keep working at it trying to get it right how do you think that is going to work it isn't. And if it isn't capitalism, because you have already agreed that it needs to be replaced, then what exactly will it be? This book has a couple of suggestions but you can go and look on the internet if you like DON'T GO AND LOOK ON THE INTERNET. It is awful, it is full of neoliberals and racists although the otter gifs are good.

neoliberal   racist   otter

What you will need

To believe that you can do anything if you put your mind to it – anything!

Just a word on intersectionality by me
Mr Olderwhiteperson. IDENTITY
POLITICS. LET ME TELL YOU YOUNG
PEOPLE A COUPLE OF THINGS. There
are other people who have thought
and written about this better you will
be shocked to learn but I think this is important and I would have
done an entire book about it but the whole idea just made me tired
we need more white men telling people what to do it has worked
really well so far.[31] The culture war has focussed on identity politics
because it is a great distraction from the class war and the economic
project of dismantling capitalism.

When I say 'a distraction' I don't mean it is less important, I mean
that the right and liberals (booo) have been happy to fight the
culture wars because they don't actually have to change anything,
they can fiddle/argue around the edges of stuff that is systemic.

Whereas, the dictatorship of the proletariat will fix racism and sexism at the same time because why the fuck not? At least that is what they told me. (Go and read some Marx, I had to. I also read a book ON Marxism by a nice man who Marxplained it very well.)

Of course, it is entirely appropriate for Mr Olderwhitecartoonist to tell you which battles you should be fighting. Turns out nice leftists like me have been banging on about the problems with capitalism and the patriarchy and racism but not actually fighting the right bits of it. But now I have written this book which is published by Rupert Murdoch and if that isn't sticking it to the man I don't know what is. I am going to go and have a lie down.

What if we let capitalism develop the forces of production enough to the point that robots do all the work, that we collectivise the robots and sit around all day eating snacks and painting pictures of pademelons. Thanks Uber and Tesla you monstrous flogs.

Under capitalism if a robot takes your job you are unemployed and also screwed, whereas under a communistrobotocracy you can go to the beach while the robot does all the things.

HOW I SURVIVED BEING A FAILED LEFTIST

There are a lot of good things about becoming a full-time political cartoonist. Foremost, politics is now officially my job, I get to sit around and draw stupid jokes about politics for A LIVING. As an industry, political cartoonists are held in some considerable regard (they should not be we are terrible). But when it actually happens to you, it is kind of interesting. Tell someone you work in the tax office or an abattoir and they will look at you funny or simply not care (unless they are a tax-avoiding cow or something). But if you tell them you are a cartoonist, they sometimes make a little excited noise and want to talk to you about it (it is awful).

For a while I thought the best bit was literally being paid to know about current affairs and what was going on in the world like a journalist does without any of the responsibility or writing things down part. But it turns out, when it comes to politics, familiarity breeds contempt. Who knew!?

I have always enjoyed and loathed Australian parliamentary politics in equal measure, mainly because of whichever particular brand of politics is on display. Like a really shit sport with unfit people. We Onthmoons have always hated the Tories. As Bob Marlton said – the worst Labor government will always be better than the best conservative government. He was right then and he is still right today bless him and if you have a different view I don't care you're a radical centrist of some sort and a lot of this is your fault go boil your head. Of course, Australian history has shown us some really gobsmackingly terrible corrupt incompetent state and federal Labor governments, and while they are simply never as brutal and cruel and shameless as the cunning tip rats on the right of politics, that is all the more dispiriting because of what should be possible e.g. HOPE. I haven't voted for them for a while but that is none of your business. These days I mainly vote for parties that promise to set circus animals free. But for the longest time I never gave up on mainstream left-wing politics because you can never give up, it is unrevolutionary. But then I gave up (just for a bit).

The world changed under us all – the emergence of the Greens and the ALP collapsing in on itself meant there was no one to barrack for any more. My faith in politics, the media's capacity to report on it and the voters' capacity to take turns doing the right thing and then buggering it up – it all finally broke (for me) when Tony Abbott came to power in Australia.

It didn't happen straight away, (it had been coming for a while anyway) but Tony really turned up the heat on the slow dispiriting cynical burn. The media's inability to do anything about it even on the rare occasions when Abbott and his cronies were held to account. It was the injustice and powerlessness of it all (how does it feel white man?), knowing that Abbott was going to make all the already terrible things worse –

to dig in on poverty and the situation of Aboriginal Australians pillage the environment and chip away at already inadequate funding for public schools and other critical institutions. Slashing funding for women's refuges while going to White Ribbon breakfasts. And the lies. Layer upon layer. But there have always been lies, it is just what governments do.

Welcome to the First Dog on the Moon Factbricator! ™

Simply feed the "truth" you don't like in the funnel and HONK! the "other side of the story" will pop out of the patented Digital Cloaca of Truth with alternative facts and added Free Speech.

FACTBRICATOR

OFF
ON
RUPERT

Perhaps there is an unspoken unacknowledged agreement with ourselves that we tolerate just enough lies to keep the world turning, but just don't make it so obvious that we have to actually face up to something, don't make it so obvious that we might have to do something or make a decision.

Then came the shit show that was Manus and Nauru – the men and women and children who were detained indefinitely in deliberately cruel conditions – that finally cracked me open. The deliberate, active brutality right before our very eyes.

Abbott was right when he said that the ALP hadn't stopped the boats, but his fascist conceit that the ONLY response was to throw desperate men and women and children into racist gulags was vile and remains so today. And it is vile that the majority of Australians are comfortable with it. Comfortable with the obvious sadistic lies.

And it didn't even stop the boats. That 'we' Australians could run actual concentrations camps in defiance of international law and human rights conventions and blah blah blah as I watched people slowly break into pieces, I was done. Piss off politics I don't like you any more. I have been quite depressed about it ever since. Then my dog died and I got fat and drank too much.

Then Turnbull was re-elected, then Brexit, then Trump. Sigh. And the left, who had been supposed to do something about all this, didn't. Where did the left go?

Co-opted by Hillary and Bill Shorten of all people. You get neoliberalism at the capitalism supermarket. They don't sell socialism there. Good heavens.

But wait. What's that noise?

The left started getting their shit together in the United States, slowly but surely. (Not the Democrats lol no.) Then Jeremy Corbyn in the UK. So that was interesting. Something is moving. Will it be enough? I doubt it. I'm happy to be proved wrong, but I'm not going to admit it because then what is the point of this book? The bottom line is that the world is going to end one way or another and saving it is a lot harder than it was before and it was already pretty hard let me tell you I've been working on it for a while. All the while, with the left's response to Trumpism and the arrival of Corbyn, the Overton window is getting downright panoramic. Will it be enough? Don't ask a cartoonist. Now that it's okay to be a Nazi it is apparently also okay to be a communist. WHO WOULD HAVE THOUGHT!?

"The left"

CHAPTER 16

The Dictatorship of
the Proletariat

What is it?

Communism! Wooooo! I'm not even joking.

According to some Marx I read (and no doubt misunderstood) socialism is the inevitable result of capitalism being so terrible and bad.

That's a relief! Although 'inevitable' doesn't mean what I want it to mean. A lot of folk spend their lives in toiling away meaninglessly for the benefit of a small group of other 'capitalists' who own all the things. It doesn't always feel like that when you're watching Netflix of course, and it sounds a bit pompous me suggesting most people's lives are meaningless struggle. My life isn't of course, it is glamorous and exciting, but not everyone can be a national treasure. I don't own the means of production either, but I do rent them at times. Would you like to buy a First Dog on the Moon tea towel? Yes you would.

Anyway it is hard to imagine we could actually do something different to capitalism as much of our culture and media spends its time explaining why water and capitalism are normal and ok and whenever something is wrong it is invariably the fault of someone whose fault it actually isn't while the perpetrators (usually the one per cent and their minions) get away scot-free those bastards. As Malcolm X said on the Instagrams that one time, 'If you're not careful, the newspapers will have you hating the people who are being oppressed, and loving the people who are doing the oppressing' and we weren't careful were we? We were not.

The idea that major social change is impossible is the preserve of the deluded. You can believe a global pandemic is possible but you can't imagine nationalising the banks how good would that be? It is less of a fantasy than

I don't know what that thing is but I don't like it

the notion that given more time and the right sort of twiddling on the levers and dials, capitalism will provide everyone with everything they need or at least a satisfactory proximity to it. Inequality is what makes capitalism go round, without it, it isn't going to be capitalism is it, but some other weird thing that rich people won't like.

The means of production and the working class and corn syrup and children in the Congo mining that stuff that goes into iphones, at some point something big has to give. Marx said a whole bunch of stuff about history and inevitability and class and I read quite a bit of it for this book and I can tell you it was quite dense and not particularly funny. To summarise: capitalism doesn't work and it is bad.

It will need to be replaced by something and that something might as well be socialism. Socialism where the state owns everything and everyone gets what they need and no more or no less but who needs more than they need? And the state is run by everyone as well. Sounds complicated and can

human nature manage it? Yes. From each according to zher ability, to each according to zher needs. Then we can replace it with communism where we all 'own' it equally and not the state, because just between you and me the state only exists to manage the struggle between worker and capitalist I'm not even joking.

Imagine if we all literally worked towards ensuring that every person on Earth had food and clean water and access to healthcare and education and that nobody went without and that we didn't chew up the environment and

natural resources to be competitive, we lived in harmony with all the bees and cows and soy plants and did exactly how much we needed and no more and no less. Imagine doing that – it is an apocalypse for our current way of life, there is no doubt about that, and how good would it be? Imagine sorting it so that robots do all the work (which capitalism is working on thanks) and we can all spend our days eating treats and looking out the window.

With capitalism, robots just take your job and make you unemployed, whereas a less horrible society would collectivise the robots that make the food and clothes and houses etc and give everyone a bunch of free time to do whatever they want with (looking out the window). How much sacrifice would you be willing to make? I'd have a crack at giving up private property for the greater good; sounds like a relief. Seriously, we don't really need our third television (actually it doesn't work properly, it would be good to offload it). And of course we are human so we would fuck it up AS LONG AS WE DIDN'T KILL EVERYONE[32] BECAUSE THAT WOULD RUIN IT. There are lots of historical reasons why it hasn't worked and plenty of people who have written about it anyway we have a lot to do.

And it seems impossible that it could be any other way – seriously, how could we replace capitalism and feudalism and so on people have tried in the past and it has worked out really badly.

The sensible folk calling for the collective ownership of all property these days don't appear to be particularly interested in popping anyone into a gulag or killing millions of humans. It quite defeats the purpose of it all.

Communism as a system of social organisation has never been truly tried and frankly I'm up for it. The good news is that it won't be the cartoonists or national treasures making the decisions, it will be everyone! A dictatorship of the proletariat, and by dictatorship I mean everyone if it is done properly. This begs the question – is it the socialism or the communism that kills all the people? Or the people doing it wrong? Governments and people who self-identified as socialist or communist have destroyed the moral authority of socialism and communism for millions of people, and the next revolution will depend on a strong and organised working class ensuring it never happens again. Because killing millions of people isn't very collective ownership of all property, is it. No it is not, and frankly, I'm not keen to get involved in anything that might result in, you know, millions of people being deliberately starved to death, like say happens now on Earth when we have enough to feed everyone but we don't. Is it the capitalism that kills people or the people who kill people, surely if we just leave the market to sort itself out (with a great many subsidies from taxpayers) then it will be glorious for everyone. I disagree and I also don't care what you think. As I said, I am going to go and live in a hole after I have written this book and I shan't be coming out until I am invited to a writers' festival.

What will happen?

Someone (not me) will organise a revolution and then I will do a few smug cartoons about it in between cleaning toilets or growing eggplants or whatever I'm rostered on to do by the collective. Or perhaps it won't happen because there is always a chance that we could lose the class war and that is exactly what it is, a war. How good is it going to be to nationalise the railways though! So good. Imagine if we all had smartphones and we owned the smartphone industry collectively so we could actually trust it, and we used our smartphones to engage in some sort of radical direct democracy type thingy.

What is the likelihood?

Idk but something has to change.

How to prepare

We're all getting hammer-and-sickle tattoos, kids!

Join the political party you hate the least, and join your union. Some say there's no parliamentary road to socialism but we need to start somewhere. Be involved in the world, start or join a community garden, a book club, a shed collective, or similar. I reckon those garden groups must be hot-beds of ecoradicalism and filled with potentially interested activist types. Start/join a group like SeaSol in Seattle (googoelge it).

Obviously, people will poo-poo these notions of collectivity and carry on about it, but I no longer care for those who poo-poo or their poo-pooery. A child dies every ten seconds from starvation – this is preventable and as a species we don't prevent it. Make all the justifications you like, I am drinking this delicious hot cup of do not @ me.

A poo pooer in the act of poo pooing

Seriously, I'm done here – is there something else we can do? Well, we're not doing it, so there you go, let's try socialism instead. Let's face it, if you bugger up doing your communism it is terrible, you might as well be ISIS – but if you bugger up your capitalism... well, let's just say that right now it appears to be working perfectly.

CHAPTER 17

Other apocoli

Here are a few other apocali that don't deserve a chapter to themselves but shouldn't go without mentioning.

Magnetic poles reversing!

What if the Earth's magnetic poles reversed? If south was north and north was south? Normally things are stable for about 10,000 to one million years (a polarity chron), although there were a couple of longer superchrons – they go for about ten million years. I don't know why it is important to have a name for the period between geomagnetic reversals and I do not care to have it explained to me. It has been 780,000 years since it last happened. IT COULD HAPPEN ANY MINUTE! What will happen? Paleomagnetists say the poles don't just go ping and switch over, it can take ages, years, or less.

A magnetic reversal may lead to 'vigorous convection' leading to widespread volcanism! But then, maybe not. This one is rated 'don't lose any sleep'. Chance of dying – teeny.

A PALEOMAGNETIST

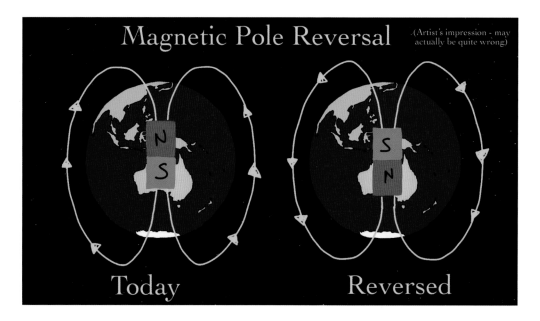

Plastic bottles

Twenty thousand plastic bottles are being bought every second. Over 480 billion plastic drinking bottles were sold in 2016 and by 2021 if we are still here it will be 583 billion. A lot of these bottles are recyclable but that doesn't mean they are being recycled. Something like 13 million tonnes of plastic ends up in the ocean every year to be ingested by sea birds fish and various other ocean going creatures, then we eat some of them. By 2050 the ocean will have more plastic than fish! People who eat seafood ingest something like 11,000 pieces of plastic a year. The plastic produced each year weighs about the same as THE ENTIRE HUMAN RACE?! This is a slower apocalypse than some of the others but it is a beaut! It is also unlike say asteroids COMPLETELY AVOIDABLE! Think about that the next time Coca Cola take a government to court to stop a container deposit recycling scheme like they did in the Northern Territory.

Grey goo!

No, not cat snot, but getting cat snot on you when a cat sneezes is absolutely apocalyptic let me tell you. Grey goo is what happens when nanotechnologists get around to building a teeny tiny (nano) self replicating robot and it self replicates OUT OF CONTROL! Adorable tiny robots! They eat the Earth! NOT SO ADORABLE NOW ARE THEY! We regret to inform you that the adorable tiny robots are killing everything. They're all munching on carbon or whatever it is and using that to build more of themselves and they just keep going and going until the Earth has been eaten and is just a bngnillion tiny robots. The idea is from Eric Drexler which is a supervillainy enough name but he is just a scientist who had an interesting idea. No one has actually built any of the these tiny robots that we know of, but if they did someone would need to invent a tiny robot stopper. Prepping wouldn't do any good and neither would having a friend who is a vet. LIKELIHOOD? Nano! Ahahah see what I did there. Chance of dying – HIGH.

Mega volcano

This is one of my favourite minor apocali. Apparently there is a supervolcano under Yellowstone National Park in the middlish bit of America that is so huge a full blown eruption would demolish half the United States. In the immediate blast zone (300 kilometres across) everything would die. Billions of tonnes of lava, ash and rock would blast into the sky, filling the atmosphere and plunging everything for thousands of kilometres into darkness.

A three-metre layer of ash would cover vast sections of the United States and two-thirds of it would be uninhabitable. Then, with the upper atmosphere full of volcano dust, winter temperatures would fall by something like 10 degrees. We would all freeze, and even if we didn't, all the crops would. THE END THANKS FOR COMING HUMANITY. Billions could die. OMG AMAZING! Chance of dying – Extreme!

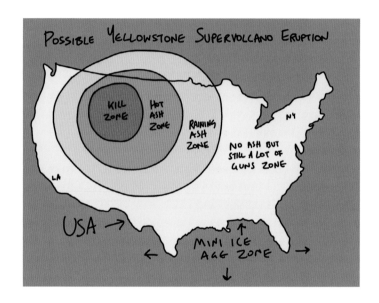

Large Hadron Collider

The Large Hadron Collider goes 'ping!' and creates a black hole everything is swallowed immediately even your carefully buried shipping container and your personalised water filtering plastic straw. The Unabomber thinks it could happen and he is not the only one. THE END. Chance of dying one hundred per cent.

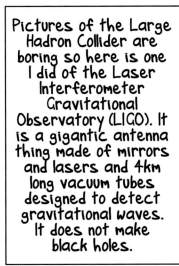

Pictures of the Large Hadron Collider are boring so here is one I did of the Laser Interferometer Gravitational Observatory (LIGO). It is a gigantic antenna thing made of mirrors and lasers and 4km long vacuum tubes designed to detect gravitational waves. It does not make black holes.

LIGO

VACUUM TUBE THINGY

HELLO

MIRROR

BEAM SPLITTER

LASER

MIRROR

MIRROR

LIGHT ARM

ONE OF THESE

4 km

GUINEA PIG
(cannot jump)

Changes in the position of the mirrors are allegedly proof of Gravitational Waves which are teeny tiny, the fraction of the width of a proton! Neither the Large Hadron Collider or LIGO can jump and when I started this book I thought Guinea Pigs couldn't jump either but wikipedia says they can. So that diagram is wrong sorry.

Meanwhile there are loads of other apocali not covered in this book and some of them are outrageous. Did you know there is 1.6 million tonnes of carbon in the permafrost? That's twice the amount of carbon causing climate change in our atmosphere right now and the PERMAFROST IS MELTING. Make of that what you will. Also, I came across the theory that the reason we haven't encountered any other life in the universe is that they all get to the same bit we are at and do themselves in. There may be loads of examples of creatures evolving to become intelligent enough to conceive of, but not quite invent, interstellar travel, but then it is too late because their climate deniers have killed them all 'accidentally'. Or something like that.

Some turtle poop

Endnote

Although this book ends here, your journey of getting ready to have a lovely time while not dying in a global catastrophe is just beginning.

Being a hardcore prepper can be weird and obsessive and anti-social, but you can say the same thing about being on Twitter, and with Twitter you don't even get a tactical spork. Serious prepping looks like a lot of hard work and a lot of lists. There's certainly nothing wrong with being ready for the unexpected, or developing emergency plans and obtaining some handy things for dealing with bad surprises – it can give one a sense of confidence and agency and even reduce the anxiety around the possibility of looming doom. I recommend it. Don't prep because you're afraid of what is coming (ALTHOUGH YOU SHOULD BE), do it so you can relax because you have a sort of 'I am ready for things' feeling. Just don't make it weird. You don't have to bury a shipping container. OR DO YOU?!

Of course if the world doesn't end you will die anyway eventually but won't have wasted any time preparing for it unless you did. If the world does end you'll be ready to survive in whatever post apocalyptic world exists (go you!) unless of course you don't make it because even though you were prepared for TERRIYAKIWAKI you were at the mall shopping when the Space Elephants arrived and detonated a nuke in the food court. RIP in peace you.

And that's why the most important part of prepping is in fact other people. Not the 'they're coming through the bedroom window with an axe' other people but the 'we're all in this together' other people because we are.

Your best chance of surviving some kind of big disaster is working with family, friends and neighbours as annoying as they might be. Community! OMG. Your particular cataclysm might be a flood or capitalism, but joining with other people is the best way to survive it, and if the cataclysm doesn't arrive you have friends now!

Of course, other people are terrible even the nice ones, which is why as I have said repeatedly, I am going to live in a hole in the ground. Maybe you don't care about that and you want to survive at all costs, be a sturdy sci-fi loner skulking through the post-apocalyptic ruins, then this book isn't for you. Pity you only found that out now I hope you at least enjoyed the pictures.

If you can imagine preparing for, let's say a global pandemic, you can imagine preparing/organising for a world where capitalism is replaced by… something else less brutal. If the adorable but flimsy arguments in this book have convinced you that an apocalypse is coming in some form anyway (or is already here) then there really isn't anything to lose by having a crack at giving capitalism the wrong end of the pineapple.

In fact, if we try and replace it, we might (might) find we have saved the world anyway! Hot diggety! It's a long shot but fuckeroo why not? What have we literally got to lose if it is all about to turn to bat guano anyway? And this is not something you can do by yourselfs. It's going to take a lot of well-meaning folk getting organised.

Everyone has a role to play in whatever is to come. For example a cartoonist might not be any use at all because how much satire are we going to need in a dystopian sentient fungusocracy?

Probably not a lot, but that doesn't mean we're just going to leave the cartoonists in the forest to be eaten alive by the panthers and lightning does it? No it doesn't. And this is really important. We are going to take any cartoonists with us and share our snacks with them because otherwise we might as well give up on being human. If there is one message to take from this book, it is that we have to save the cartoonists even if it means sacrificing ourselves. Did I say that out loud?

So why not use the time we have left – however much that really is and who knows – to make the world a better place and join the struggle to put capitalism in the bin.

The reality is I am not ready for a global pandemic or any of its friends. To do the research for this book I bought a military grade spork and hand-powered chainsaw on ebay but I wouldn't call myself ready. There are some tools in the shed and quite a few tins of soup in the pantry nobody has gotten around to eating but what about the heart medicine for the little dog and the Prozac for the big dog and if we have to take the cat as well she always poops in the cat carry box so we would probably bug in because where would we go anyway? I don't know.

The world is so lovely, so full of glorious things and my tiny words can't come near it. I love it ferociously. Sometimes it is too big and too full of sadness and horror, but how good is being alive! I reckon it is wonderful (when it isn't terrible) and I hope it is for you too. Is that enough? That everyone and every thing should have a chance at being in the world the way they want because what else are you going to do? That's what I'm working on. Good luck with it all.

HERE IS A HELPFUL LIST OF WHAT PEOPLE CAN DO TO PREPARE FOR THE END OF THE WORLD AND MAKE IT A BETTER PLACE IN THE MEANTIME OR INSTEAD OF IT ENDING.

JOIN YOUR UNION

JOIN THE POLITICAL PARTY YOU HATE THE LEAST

LEARN TO ODOURLESS COOK

ADOPT A DOG

YOUR NEW DOG IS LONELY ADOPT ANOTHER DOG

VOLUNTEER SOMEWHERE THAT NEEDS VOLUNTEERS

BECOME A COMMUNIST

JOIN AN ASYLUM SEEKER SUPPORT ORGANISATION

STOP MANSPLAINING

STOP BEING OFFENDED WHEN PEOPLE MAKE JOKES ABOUT MANSPLAINING

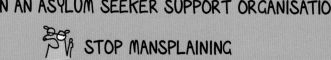

HELP FIND A WAY TO SLOW/STOP/AMELIORATE GLOBAL WARMING OUR CHOICE IS BETWEEN ACTION OR DEATH I'M NOT EVEN JOKING

Glossawary

Here are some of the words and phrases you have to use when you are a Prepper otherwise nobody will know what you are talking about.

Prepper: Someone who does all the things suggested in this book and dies anyway because all their stuff will run out eventually and they can't live in the forest using only their wits to survive like a survivalist.

Survivalist: Someone who can live in the forest using only their wits to survive eating sticks and dirt like an annoying beardy Bear Grylls sort of person.

SHTF: Shit hits the fan.

TEOTWAWKI: The end of the world as we know it.

WROL: Without rule of law.

WOL: Friend of Winnie the Pooh.

GOOD: Get out of Dodge (flee).

#10 cans: A popular size of can for food storage.

BOB: Bug out bag – a bag for bugging out with.

BOL: Bug out location – a hopefully secure location for bugging out to with your bug out bag.

BOV: Bug out vehicle – a vehicle to drive to the location you are bugging out to with your bug out bag.

BAB: Big arse baboon don't run into any of these! They will kill you.

HEMP: High Altitude Electromagnetic Pulse (yes I know high altitude is two words but I didn't make that one up – and electromagnetic is one word but it gets an E and an M I didn't hear anyone complaining about that).

ELE: Extinction Level Event (bad).

EDC: Everyday carry, which is a bag you take with you everywhere all the time just in case. It has a spork and a lifestraw and some other things inside.

MRE: Meals Ready to Eat like the ones the army get, or you can make them yourself by getting ripe bananas or rocks if you are really hungry.

FAK: First aid kit.

FUK: The world is ending!

Casserole: Delicious stew of the things you make stew from – sometimes tastes like chicken.

Cassowary: Large prehistoric death bird that hates you – not like a chicken at all.

Cache: Hidden stash of stuff like food or clean underwear.

Coronal Mass Ejection: Sounds ruder than it is – it's just the sun having a bad day.

Faraday Cage: Keep everyone safe from ferocious Faradays by making sure they are in a cage.

Solar oven: Use the sun to cook stuff – apparently it works.

Two is one and one is none: The idea that you need a spare of everything because for example if you lose your torch at night you can't see in the dark to find it without a torch.

INCH: I'm never coming home.

LUNCH: is cancelled the world is ending.

HALT: Humidity, Air, Light, Temperature – these are the enemies of your stored foods. Keep them completely away from these things until just before you pop the food in your mouth.

TBCH: To be completely honest.

IMHO: In my humble (and correct) opinion.

Homesteading: A lifestyle of self-sufficiency.

Seasteading: Creating permanent dwellings/islands at sea outside the control of any government.

Waterbob: A guy named Bob who lives on a seastead!

Waterbob (also): A large plastic doover for storing water in your bathtub, no seriously it is a huge bag and you put it in the tub and fill it with water and it keeps the dust off it.

Acknowledgemints ahahahahha

This book would not have been possible without the selfless endeavours of

B Saurus, Ruby, Molly, Roy, Chu Chu, Peanut, Marieke Hardy, Sophie Black, Michael Williams, Gabrielle Jackson, @Marrowing, Sam Long, Kylie Grant, Lucy, Henry and Paul, Jon Kudelka, Matt Groening, Eatenfish and everyone at ABC Books especially Lachlan, Jane, Brigitta and Jude.

Also thanks to Jonathon "Mr Frog" Green, Sally Heath, Chris Roberts, Lenore Taylor, Kath Viner, Janet Galbraith, Liam Hogan, David Paris, "Dan Nolan", Ben Harris-Roxas, David Mallard, Jason Wilson, Adrian Dodd, Scont Bridges, Evan Beaver, Gleb Fuller, Nick Evershed, Lucy Clark, @murpharoo, Gabrielle Chan, Elle Hunt, Ben Doherty, Paul Farrell, Mel Davey, Calla Wahlquist, Paul Karp, Will Woodward, Mikey Slezak, Svetlana Stankovic, Dave Earley, Emily Wilson, Helen Davidson, Chris Endrey, Nick Feik, Michelle Bennet, Liv Nenna, Scott Ludlam, Henry Cook, Dejan Stojanovic, Mark Holdsworth, Peter Gordon and Denis Bicer. Also also thanks to Volker, Berta and the mob at Tinning St, Bernard Keane, Byron Koester, Tom Jellett, Jeff Sparrow, @Mathiaus, @Darovda, Anthony Morgan who's joke got edited out, Mike Bowers, Fiona Katauskas, Paul Webster, Guy Rundle, Lesley Podesta, Louise Lovett, Carl Rayson and Barbara Evans. John, Jeremy and Simon Marlton.

Also Luke Beveridge who didn't do anything for the book but coached the Western Bulldogs to a flag in 2016 so he will be in every book from now on.

Endnotes

1   Ahahaha no you won't.

2   Do not read the disclaimer on page 190.

3   It's in the glossary.

4   Australian Broadcasting Corporation.

5   Nazi tapeworms burst through the floor.

6   I did not take it out of the book. But it is very dark indeed.

7   The book not the tv show.

8   'I'll take care of it, Luke said. And because he said it instead of her, I knew he meant kill. That is what you have to do before you kill, I thought. You have to create an it, where none was before. You do that first, in your head, and then you make it real. So that's how they do it, I thought. I seemed never to have known that before.' Excerpt From: Margaret Atwood, *The Handmaid's Tale*.

9   A mass of refugees and looters who will leave the cities sometime after TAKITWAKITA.

10 This is actually a real spork but I have no idea if they use them in the army.

11 It really isn't a joke. Go to www.firstshoponthemoon.com

12 Self-appointed

13 Eschatological

14 Actually our motto is 'It wasn't so bad we couldn't drink it' but that doesn't have the same gravitas.

15 According to the internet.

16 No, it is in the glossary.

17 Remember cheques?! I do! Good times.

18 Not rhyming slang just apt.

19 Milkshake duck joke (which is now a meme) courtesy of @pixelatedboat

20 Or you don't more to the point.

21 SPOILER ALERT!

22 Seriously, it is a remarkable game and this book doesn't really have any room for sport and we probably won't play much of it when the end of the world comes, but go dogs!

23 A Scientist.

24 TSCHTFBT! TS!

25 My preschool! One of my earliest memories is nailing two bits of wood together crossways to make a plane but I nailed it to the wooden cable reel we are using as a workbench then Dad arrives to take me home but my plane is nailed to the bench!

26 Whatever that means.

27 I could tell that it wasn't very good because they hired me as a cartoonist.

28 Whatever that means.

29 No we will eat them.

30 It will all trickle down so much it will be a rising tide that will lift all boats unless they have a hole in them or maybe you don't have a boat, maybe what you have is a pair of floaties, how is that going to work.

31 Said the Caucasian fellow as he went on to explain that…

32 LIKE CAPITALISM IS TRYING TO DO.

33 Not really every effort, more like some efforts. A few small efforts that were tried. One tiny effort that tripped over and scraped its knee so then gave up and went home.

General Disclaimer

Every[33] effort has been made to make sure this book is mostly complete and accurate, however there will be mistakes, we are only human. This book is a work of fiction (except the bits that are true which is most of it) and it should ONLY be used as a GENERAL and NOT even then VERY GOOD guide to the subject matter which is how not to die in case of an existential threat or small household emergency.

The purpose of this book is to entertain and frighten, not to inform. We are not even experts we just googled it. And the googles we found weren't experts either just random weirdies on the internet with some really terrible websites – you should have a look. If you find an alternative fact, feel free to leave a smug know-it-all comment below ahahaha. No wait, you can't, it is a book not a stupid cartoon on the internet.

Accordingly, we have no liability or responsibility to anyone or thing thick-witted enough to suffer loss or damage alleged or otherwise that is or isn't caused directly or indirectly by doing or not doing the extremely stupid things in this book. Ever.

The content herein is based on personal experiences (primarily of reading things on the internet) although we did try a few things in the back yard (I hurt my leg) and isn't it nice to get out in the country occasionally? We can recommend it but only with a professional driver and an armoured vehicle. This document should not be treated as teaching material unless you want to teach people how to die in the woods from avoidable accidents.

Of course, there is a serious point to be made in this book but to find out what that is you will actually have to read it.

The End

First Dog on the Moon aka Andrew Marlton is the Walkley award-winning political cartoonist for The Guardian Australia. First Dog has written and illustrated various books including this one, illustrated numerous others and is currently working on more exciting projects than you can poke a stick at including another stage show and more books. *First Dog on the Moon's Guide to Modern Living* used to air weekly on ABC Radio National and people still ask him about it, and don't forget there are award winning shows that appear occasionally at the Melbourne International

Comedy Festival. Mr Onthemoon is also currently the official cartoonist for the Western Bulldogs AFL Team. A self-described 'National Treasure', First Dog spends most days working at the First Dog on the Moon Institute, a bipartisan think tank in sunny Brunswick, Melbourne. You can buy First Dog on the Moon merchandise at the firstshoponthemoon.com, and a large percentage of the proceeds from all merchandise sales goes to assist cartoonist First Dog on the Moon – actually all of it does, which is nice.